HOW I OVERCAME BEING BULLIED

DAVID REMINGTON

HOW I OVERCAME BEING BULLIED

DAVID REMINGTON

Published by

Cathedral City, California

2026

How I Overcame Being Bullied
Copyright © 2026 by David Remington

All rights reserved. No part of this publication may be reproduced, distributed, or transmitted in any form or by any means, including photocopying, recording, or other electronic or mechanical methods, without the prior written permission of the publisher, except as permitted by U.S. copyright law. For permission requests, contact the publisher.

For privacy reasons, some names, locations, and dates may have been changed.

First paperback edition August 2025
Reprint February 2026

Book design by AquaZebra.com

Library of Congress Control Number: 2025908903

ISBN: 978-1-954604-18-6 (paperback)

Published by AquaZebra
35070 Maria Rd
Cathedral City, CA 92234
aquazebra@gmail.com

Warning: explicit sexual content and drug use;
reader discretion advised.

Dedication

I would like to dedicate this book to Margaret Beaman. Thank you for encouraging me to write my story. Without you this book would not have been written. Thank you for being a good friend and an ally to the gay community.

With love,
David

Table of Contents

Introduction

When I was in college, I took a weekend seminar offered through Landmark Education. It was called The Forum. Over the course of three days, we learned many techniques about how to let go of our past and be in the present. One of the questions posed by the leader went something like this (paraphrasing): "If you were walking down the street, and a window fell off a tall building and hit you, would that be your fault?"

Now, I don't recall the entire discussion after that question. It had something to do with taking responsibility for choosing to be on that street at the exact moment the window fell down. What it did for me was open my mind to the idea that maybe I was responsible for having been bullied. Did I allow it to happen? But I wasn't ready, nor did I have all the information I needed to really take accountability for what happened. However, it planted a seed in my mind that would germinate nearly ten years later.

At that time, I was still living under the impression that the bullying simply ended once I graduated high school. Since it was over, I thought it was best to just leave it alone. After all, it was something I never admitted to anyone. I just didn't discuss it. For all intents and purposes, it was my dirty little secret.

And so, it stayed until I found myself in my mid-thirties, sitting outside an elementary school, absolutely petrified to walk through the door. I was afraid that a bunch of eight- and nine-year-old students were going to call me a "faggot." I realized I had a problem. Clearly, what I thought had ended when I graduated was still with me. Deep in the pit of my stomach was all the fear, anger and shame I had buried away the day I graduated from high school.

I decided to write this book for several reasons. The first is that most often, when the topic of bullying is discussed, the focus is often on the bully; what makes them abusive, why they behave that way, and how we can help the bully to stop bullying. The people who are often left out of the conversation are the people who get bullied. After all, aren't we the ones who bring on the attention? It seems that, not only are we allowed to slip through the cracks of the system when we are bullied, but years later we find no space to discuss our experience and how it's impacted our lives.

The other reason I'm writing is because I take issue with the phrase "it gets better." I think we can all agree that not being called a faggot every day is almost instantly refreshing. However, to suggest that life just somehow gets better after graduation from high school is like putting a Band-Aid on a bullet hole. It simply does not address the enormous amount of trauma we are left to process after the bullying ends. Depending on the severity of your experience, you may be left with undiagnosed PTSD, anxiety, and/or major depression. These do not just go away. Left untreated, the damage can result in ruined lives, destroyed families and drug or alcohol abuse.

Finally, I am writing this book for you. For anyone who has ever been bullied. When I got home that day after I was afraid to walk into that elementary school, I googled "long-term consequences of bullying." Let me tell you, I didn't find much. Virtually no scientific studies have ever been conducted on anyone who has experienced severe bullying. I found this deeply disturbing. That was the moment I knew I had to chart this course on my own. It took me almost twenty years to recover from the bullying I experienced all through school, and I know I'm not the only one. I wrote this book to help anyone who has ever been bullied. It is possible to recover. It is possible to take your life back. The first step is admitting that it happened to you. I know for most people, that is the hardest part.

Long-Term Consequences

I turned off the car engine and suddenly began to panic. My heart was pounding, sweat beading on my forehead. I was shaking. I had a sinking feeling in the pit of my stomach. I was terrified, afraid of what might happen when I walked into that elementary school.

I was parked outside Roskruge Elementary School in Tucson, Arizona, to meet with children who had been selected by their guidance counselor to participate in a mentoring program called Big Brothers Big Sisters. I was the newly hired program coordinator. And here I was, thirty-five years old, terrified of walking into an elementary school.

But why?

Attempting to calm myself down, I tried some deep breathing exercises. Then I asked myself, *David, what are you so afraid of?* My answer was, *When I walk into that elementary school, every one of those kids is going to point at me and yell, "Faggot!"* Believe it or not, that's exactly what I was afraid was going to happen.

I had always worked in retail after graduating from college, but for a brief time I accepted a position with Big Brothers Big Sisters of Tucson. You may not be familiar with this organization. It provides mentoring for children in need of a strong role model. Most of the children involved have only one parent or are living with a guardian, although a few children came from two-parent households. Typically, the "Big" (the mentor) would meet with their "Little" (the child) once a week for a community activity of their choosing.

The program I was hired to manage was called "site based." The "Bigs" and their "Littles" met weekly at the school for an after-school program. My job was to coordinate with school counselors to help identify children in need and recruit new Bigs (volunteers.) I would introduce the two and support them through site visits while they were together.

I spent the first month of the job on the phone with school counselors and interviewing adult volunteers. The time came when I had to do my first school visit to meet some of the children. I arrived at the school, parked my car, and had a massive panic attack.

Fortunately, I managed to calm myself down just enough to get out of the car and walk into the school. To my surprise, the children were happy and excited to see me. I was completely relieved. It turned out that these kids were genuinely enthusiastic about getting a Big, and I was the one who got to feel all that excitement.

So, you're probably thinking, *Okay, so you conquered your fear. What's the big deal?* The big deal was, that night when I got home, I could no longer live under the illusion that the bullying had ended when I graduated from high school. The level of fear I felt in the car was more than palpable. I realized that the childhood trauma of being bullied was still with me. Deep in the core of my being, I felt like I had a monster living inside me and I didn't know how to get rid of it. I also couldn't go back to pretending that everything was okay. If a thirty-something-year-old man was afraid to walk into an elementary school, something was very wrong.

That night I googled "long term consequences of bullying," but I didn't find much. At that time, no studies had been conducted on the long-term effects of bullying. No scientific information was available on how childhood bullying impacts your adult life.

I started looking for brain research. I wanted to know what was happening in my brain while I was being bullied. Most people understand, that between birth and twenty-seven years of age, our brains develop in a way that sets the stage for the rest of our lives. Although I learned it is possible to grow and regrow new brain cells later in life, once the basic functions are set in during adolescence, you're stuck with them.

But how does getting bullied impact the brain? Research has been conducted on "fight or flight" mode, but I'm not going to explain all of that here because I'm not a scientist. I barely made it through high school. How did I have time to study when all I could think about was how to avoid getting my ass kicked at the end of the day? But I do want to point out here that, when your brain is in "fight or flight" mode, it produces an extra amount of adrenaline. This is an extraordinary experience that puts additional stress on the normal brain functions. But what if your childhood was spent every day in "fight or flight" mode? Could this have had a negative impact on my brain development—on the brain that I'm stuck with for the rest of my life? Could this be a consequence of perpetual bullying?

That bit of knowledge was all I needed to begin my journey into examining my life to determine what those long-term consequences could be.

I realized something else when I was reading about the brain and its "fight or flight" function. You could say I had a paradigm shift into how I perceived myself. This shift occurred because I had always thought of myself as a coward. I was afraid to fight, and so I ran. I never perceived myself as a courageous person. Then I learned that the brain is a smart machine. It sees things we can't see with our eyes. It perceives things that we're unaware of, and it functions in ways that are unknown on a conscious level. When we are in a fight or flight situation, our brain quickly investigates and *decides for us*. Although it may *seem* as if we are deciding to fight or run, our brain is able to assess the situation with far more information and then puts our bodies into motion just as it seems we are making the decision ourselves. With that knowledge, I had to recognize that my brain was making the decision for me. My brain was evaluating the situation: We were outnumbered. To survive, we *had to* run, again and again.

Because when I really thought about it, *the bullies never really "got me."* They were never able to beat me up. Don't get me wrong; just about every day, I'd get an invitation from one of them to get my ass kicked after school, but somehow, I always managed to outsmart them. I was hiding somewhere, watching as they waited for me to show up, or I figured out how to get myself back on the bus without them seeing me. Maybe I wasn't such a chicken after all.

When I realized that they never "got me," I began to feel a little braver. That was the paradigm shift I was talking about. Maybe—just maybe—I had a little more courage than I thought. Just enough, in fact, to face my past and forgive myself for always running. Because maybe my brain was a little smarter than me.

While having this seemingly life-changing experience, I couldn't help noticing something else. I was sitting in my house where I lived with my husband, in Tucson, Arizona, more than three thousand miles from where I grew up. Then it hit me.

When I went away to college, I decided to have the experience of being far away from home. I don't know if I chose the University of New Mexico or it happened to be the only college that accepted me. (Again, not the brightest student.) Regardless, I went to New Mexico for college and after graduation lived there for a while with my boyfriend, Jerry. He was from Roswell, New Mexico, and always dreamed of living in New England. We made the decision together to move to Rhode Island and be around my family.

It all sounded great, planning it out in our living room in Albuquerque, but once we got to Rhode Island, I felt uneasy.

I started working at the new Providence Place mall. I was an assistant manager at J. Crew. During the first holiday season, an older woman who was shopping with her daughter walked up to me and asked, "Are you David Remington?"

"Yes," I replied.

She turned to her daughter and said, "Look, Stacy, it's little David Remington from St. Augustine." Her daughter had been in my elementary school class. She looked down at me—she was shorter than me, but still looked down at me—and said, "Oh, it's you."

I was mortified. Here I was, a college graduate, starting my life over, and it felt like I was in elementary school all over again.

Even though I hadn't made a conscious decision at that time, as soon as I had a chance, I made up some stupid excuse to tell Jerry I could no longer be his boyfriend. I broke up with him and moved to Arizona. I couldn't tell Jerry the real reason—that I was still afraid of anyone finding out who I really was—a product of lifelong bullying, a kind of human punching bag.

I didn't even want Jerry to know, and he was the love of my life. We had no boundaries with each other. Jerry is still the only person with whom I've felt comfortable taking a dump in the same room. He is also the only boyfriend who has ever given me a Dutch oven. (In case you aren't familiar with a Dutch oven, it's when you fart in bed with someone and then pull the covers over their head.) Jerry and I laughed A LOT. We always had a great time, like two best friends hanging out after school. But that bond still wasn't strong enough for me to reveal my deepest secret to him.

My decision to move over three thousand miles away from where I grew up was because I never wanted to run into another person who knew what happened to me in school. I didn't want anyone to know how gravely I'd been shamed by the bullying, and I certainly didn't want to be reminded of it by any of my former classmates. So, I left. In essence, I was running from my past, but now it seemed like it was starting to catch up to me.

Not only could being bullied have impacted my early brain development, but now, later in life, it seemed to be impacting major life decisions. I had made an unconscious decision to move thousands of miles away because I didn't want to ever run into anyone who knew about my past. It apparently did have long-term consequences. Now I began to wonder what other decisions I was making because of it.

Little Brother

I had a lot of information to process and unpack, so I started seeing a therapist. I wanted to talk about my experiences of being bullied.

I remained afraid of these eight- and nine-year-olds. I decided to volunteer as a mentor with Big Brothers Big Sisters, the agency I was working for.

One boy in the group was named Matthew. He attended one of the elementary schools where I managed a "site-based" program. Matthew was enrolled in the program, but he didn't have a Big yet. Matthew was in second grade at that time.

One afternoon I was scheduled to conduct the community-based introduction with his Big as a favor to the community match support specialist, since I happened to be scheduled at his school that day. I met Matthew and his mom while we were waiting for the Big to show up. The volunteer was significantly late. I made a joke with Matthew about how much more punctual he was than his future Big Brother. Matthew replied, "Well, I've had it on my calendar for two weeks!" He then burst into tears and ran into his mother's arms. His reaction was heartbreaking.

When I learned that the Big had changed his mind about participating, I went back to the office and reported it per protocol. I thought about volunteering to become Matthew's Big Brother, but I didn't want to do it simply out of pity. I had already completed an application and passed all the background checks required to participate. Yet I still wondered if I'd be any good at it, or if he'd be the right Little for someone with my history.

When we found a new Big for Matthew, I was relieved. They were matched and things seemed to be going well. I often ran into the boy when I was visiting his friends who were involved in the program. I'd always check in with him just to see how things were going, and he always seemed excited to see me. When he saw me coming up the sidewalk, he'd yell to me from the schoolyard, "Hey, David, watch me kick this ball!" He was a sweet, well-mannered boy, and he seemed happy with the way things were going.

Then the unthinkable happened. Matthew's Big Brother was a student at the University of Arizona. He was participating in the program for class credit. After the semester was over, he ditched Matthew and never showed up again. Matthew was devastated, and so was I. I couldn't believe someone would be so cruel and selfish with such an adorable child. I knew it was time for me to step in and become Matthew's Big Brother. I may not have known exactly what to do or how to do it, but I knew I wouldn't break his heart.

I went to his community match support person and asked if I could read the application his mother had filled out. She was looking for a Big who could take Matthew to play sports or go to sporting events. This I knew I couldn't do; I hated sports. Maybe it had something to do with always getting picked last, or maybe I'm just not athletic, which is *why* I always got picked last.

But I proceeded to call his mom and expressed interest in being Matthew's Big Brother. The first thing I told her was that I was gay. I went on to say that I'd be happy to be Matthew's Big Brother, but that playing sports was out of the question. I would do other things with him like go to the movies, take him out to eat, or help him with homework. It turned out she had no problem with any of that. She was thrilled that I wanted to be a part of Matthew's life and supported my decision.

By this time, Matthew was in the third grade. We had our formal introduction at the Big Brothers, Big Sisters of Tucson office located in downtown Tucson, Arizona. I still have the photo that was taken at that introduction. I was excited to participate in the program but also nervous. Excited about the idea of being a "father figure" to a child whose father passed away when he was still a baby, but nervous because, being gay and in my early thirties, this was probably the closest I'd ever come to being a father. Additionally, I didn't want to screw things up for him the way my father did with my sister and me.

I told myself I would do the opposite of what my father did. When I was planning our first meeting outside of school, I asked myself, *What would my father do?* Well, my father never had a plan when we got together. We'd always end up sitting in his car in the parking lot of a drugstore after he'd taken us inside and bought each of us a candy bar. So, I made a plan. There was a pizza place across the street from Matthew's elementary school. I decided I would pick him up from school and take him out for pizza.

Then I wondered, *What will I talk about?* So, I asked myself, *What would my father talk about?* My father would always complain to us about what a bitch our mother was and how her two sisters were trying to tear the family apart. So, I told myself I would not complain or talk about my life unless he asked me about it. Then I wondered, *Well, what would we talk about?* So, I told myself I could ask him three questions: how his day went, how he was feeling, and what was on his mind. I would leave the rest to him. I also thought it would be a good idea to have something to play with just in case the conversation was light. So, I bought a few age-appropriate children's card games for us to play while we waited for the pizza.

I'm happy to say Matthew is now attending graduate school and is currently employed as a middle school teacher in Tucson. Although I have lived in three states since we were first matched, I maintained contact with him throughout by calling him regularly and sending him cards for the holidays and his birthday. Although it was tough after I moved to Palm Springs and began to struggle with my addiction to crystal meth, I was honest with him when I was struggling, because I didn't ever want to talk to him on the phone when I was high. Admittedly, there were about four years when I didn't have much contact other than sending him cards. I even remember one birthday when, because of my addiction, I missed sending him a birthday card. Boy, did he let me have it! I was heartbroken when he scolded me for missing his birthday, so I haven't missed one since. Although I missed his high school graduation, I was there when he graduated from the University of Arizona. I'm thrilled when he calls me to see how I'm doing or tells me about how his job is going.

The greatest compliment I've ever received was back when Matthew and I were having pizza after school. He had gotten up from the table to use the bathroom while I was paying the bill. An older woman had been sitting next to us. As I was paying, she got up to leave, turned to me, and said, "I just wanted to let you know, you're a really great dad."

I was stunned. I immediately wanted to start explaining how I wasn't really his dad but thought that could get kind of dicey. After all, what's a single gay guy doing with a little boy in a pizza shop? Instead, I just said, "Thank you," and let the woman be on her way.

During the five years I was matched with Matthew, we saw each other about once a week. After the great recession of 2008 the agency suffered major financial cutbacks and my position was eliminated. I returned to my retail career at Banana Republic. I was eventually promoted from the store in Tucson to a larger store in Las Vegas.

At our last get-together in Tucson, I told Matthew I would be a part of his life for as long as he wanted me to be. Matthew is still the joy of my life and I'm so glad I made that decision to be a mentor.

Fag

When I was growing up, my sister and I were mostly left to our own devices. She and I were called "latchkey kids." We lived on the third floor of a tenement house on Garfield Avenue in Providence, Rhode Island. It was located on the line between Elmhurst (a working-class neighborhood) and Smith Hill (otherwise known as "the ghetto"). My sister and I attended St. Augustine Elementary School in a nicer neighborhood called Mt. Pleasant.

Because our parents were going through a divorce, our father moved out of the house and our mother worked several jobs, so we took the city bus to school. We were the only kids at our school who took the city bus. Most of the students either walked to school or got rides from their parents. I am pretty sure we were the only students there who came from a broken home, and I wouldn't be surprised if we were the poorest.

I remember thc first time I was called a "fag" at school. It was in first grade, and I had a crush on Katie. She was the prettiest girl in first grade. She had cute blonde hair, cut just above the shoulders with bangs. She often wore it pulled back with a headband to match her outfit. Katie also dressed the best. Her outfits were well coordinated and charming. One day I kissed this adorable blond girl on the cheek, which, apparently, was taboo in first grade. Steven caught me kissing Katie and called me a "fag." I didn't even know what a fag was, but it sounded awful. I didn't know how to respond. I wasn't raised in a home where name calling was acceptable or even tolerated. As a result, I remained silent. That silence was perceived as permission to call me a fag over and over. Steven's cousin, Vinny, caught on to the name calling, and soon multiple students were chiming in. "Fag, fag, fag" was all I ever heard.

Without going into more miserable details, I'll just say that the bullying started in first grade and continued to get worse every year. In eighth grade, our conservative Catholic school decided to provide us a one-hour sexual education class, conducted by an individual from outside the school. We met in the library, and students were asked to write anonymous questions on a piece of paper and place them in a hat. The instructor read each question aloud and answered it.

One student's question read, "Can you get AIDS from buttfucking?" Everyone burst into laughter except me. I must have looked pale or upset because before the instructor answered the question he said to me, "Would you like to go get a drink of water?" I nodded my head and slowly walked towards the library door. I remember reaching for the door handle and fainting.

I woke up sitting in a chair as my sweater was being pulled over my head by my teacher. I could hear everyone around me laughing. I passed out again and woke up lying on a couch in the teacher's lounge with my only two friends, Denise and Jackie, staring at me.

I asked, "What happened?"

They both replied, "You passed out."

"Oh," I said.

Then they proceeded to tell me that they couldn't be my friend anymore because Stacy (the same Stacy I ran into at J. Crew years later) told them that if they continued to be my friends, they were going to get ridiculed as I was. They both walked out of the room and left me there alone. I was completely stunned. On the one hand, I could totally understand why they abandoned me, but on the other, I was deeply hurt. Now I had no one to be friends with. The next day I came to school to find my desk covered with "Dizzy Dave" Garbage Pail Kid stickers.

And that, my friends, "sums up" my elementary school experience.

Monday through Friday was miserable, so I lived for the weekends. On Saturday mornings, I'd wake up at five o'clock to enjoy as much of the day as possible without being called a "faggot" every minute. I'd jump out of bed and turn on the TV just as broadcasting began. (This was before the advent of 24-hour cable television.) The first cartoon on Saturday was *David and Goliath*. I'd watch cartoons until about noon, then return to my room where I'd listen to my albums and read. Mysteries were my favorite. I read every one of the *Hardy Boys* mysteries and a few of my sister's *Nancy Drews*. My favorite albums were my Disney storybook albums. My mother told me that's how I taught myself to read at a young age. I would listen to the albums over and over, following along in the storybook accompanying the album. My favorite was *Cinderella*.

Growing up, my three role models were Cinderella, Snow White and Mary Poppins. What these three women taught me was this lesson: Does your life suck? Are people being mean to you? Are your parents ignoring you? Do you find yourself talking to animals instead of people? No problem! Just sing a little song, do a little dance, and everything is going to work out fine.

I loved talking to the animals. We didn't have woodland animals in Providence like they had in the storybooks. On Saturday afternoons, I'd take my Cinderella storybook out to the front porch and read it to the pigeons and squirrels sitting in the tree in front of our house. They seemed to enjoy it, and I loved it when they hopped closer to me. I felt just like Cinderella making friends with the animals—hoping someday my prince would come and save me from my miserable childhood!

Our parents were never around. Our father's visitation day was Saturday, and he rarely showed up. If he did, he was usually several hours late, leaving us maybe an hour or two of his time. Our mother worked several jobs, and three nights a week we were shipped off to our aunt and uncle's house in the suburbs of Warwick, about twenty minutes south of Providence. This wasn't so bad. They had a nicer house and were the first people in the state of Rhode Island to get cable TV. We never had cable at home; our mother couldn't afford it.

I wanted to be kidnapped. Mornings I would sit at the table eating my cereal, looking at the kid's pictures on the milk carton. Back then, missing children's pictures were placed on the back of milk cartons. I would look at those kids and think, *Gee, why can't that be me?* At least someone wanted those kids. I wanted to be loved and to feel like I was wanted. It seemed to me that those kids had it good because someone must have really wanted them if they were kidnapped. I had no problem walking near empty vans and standing at the bus stop on Smith Street in Providence (sometimes actually holding out my thumb), just waiting for someone to scoop me up.

It never happened.

High school didn't get any better. Actually, that's not entirely true. My first year of high school, I attended Bishop Connely in Fall River, Massachusetts. It wasn't so bad. I didn't get bullied that first year.

During my last year at St. Augustine's, my mother began to build a house for herself in Swansea, Massachusetts. She'd never had that kind of money before, but she'd put herself on a long waitlist for a government subsidized mortgage program, "farmer's mortgage" they called it, and finally her turn came around. Applicants got the money they needed to build the house and, if they sold it, they would pay it back. However, the house had to be built or purchased in a town which had fewer than 10,000 residents, and it couldn't be built on land that had previously been farmland. So, we found a plot of land that met the regulations in Swansea, a rural town not far from us, and by the time I graduated from eighth grade we were ready to move into our new home. A small ranch house with three bedrooms, and one bath. It was a humongous change, having grown up in an urban slum and then moving to the country. The closest Catholic school, a Jesuit high school, was in Fall River, a town slightly smaller than Providence and about a twenty-five-minute drive away. I felt comfortable there and didn't have a problem making new friends. My mother joined a carpool group of other moms from our area, so I got to meet kids who didn't know my history.

During my freshman year, my mom thought it would be a good idea if I got a part-time job. I was able to get a worker's permit in Massachusetts as soon as I turned 15. I got hired as a busboy at a restaurant down the street from our new house called The Sportsman II. (I guess there was another Sportsman I somewhere, but I couldn't tell you for sure.) I hated the job.

However, I found one of the other busboys rather fascinating. His name was Philip. We were both freshman in high school, but he attended the local public school, Joseph Case High School. He was flamboyant, studied theater and dance, and liked to perform ballet moves around the dining room. I was fascinated by his flamboyancy. I couldn't believe someone could act so "gay" so unapologetically. He liked to follow me into the bathroom, showed me his dick and asked to see mine. I was a shy kid and a little apprehensive about showing him my dick, but he made me feel comfortable, so I had no problem doing it.

We exchanged phone numbers and started hanging out in between shifts. I got fired two weeks later. They just took me off the schedule without an explanation. My mom had to go in and talk to the manager about why I wasn't getting scheduled. The manager said I ate too much ice cream out of the freezer and asked the other busboys to do my job for me. Both offenses were probably true, but no one had told me I couldn't do those things.

Anyway, Philip and I continued our friendship outside of work. Swansea was a wooded community. Philip and I didn't live that far from each other; we just had to cut through a patch of the woods to get from my house to his. We would talk on the phone, then hang up and start walking toward each other's house, often meeting up in the woods.

One day Philip decided we should play Truth or Dare. I had never played that before and was a little scared of what might happen, but I agreed because we were friends. The dares started innocently enough. He said, "I dare you to show me your dick" and "I dare you to kiss me."

Then I upped the ante and said, "I dare you to suck my dick." To which he replied, "I'll suck yours if you suck mine." I thought about it for a second and said, "Okay." I had never sucked a dick before and didn't really know what to do. I remember putting my mouth over his dick trying not to get my lips on it. It was the first time with a dick in my mouth, so I had no idea what I was doing.

Philip and I continued to hang out and play games throughout our whole freshman year. Then my last report card came in and my grades at school weren't so great. Again, not the brightest student. My high school wanted to hold me back a year and make me repeat freshmen year, which I flat-out refused. My mom took me down to the Swansea public school system, and they said if I attended Joseph Case I could still graduate in three years.

It was a tough decision because I was afraid to go to public school. Philip used to tell me about how he got bullied at school, and after having a year off from bullying, I didn't want to go back. However, I still hated school and the thought of having to do an extra year was worse than the thought of getting bullied again. So, I decided I would attend Joseph Case, but I had to ditch Philip first. I figured if people knew we were friends I would be an easy target to get bullied. So, I stopped calling him and basically ditched him all summer.

Then the first day of school came. My plan completely backfired in my face. Because I still got called a faggot on day one, and now, I had also lost my only friend, Philip. He would glare at me when we passed in the hallway and told all his theater friends not to hang out with me. What an idiot I had been! I completely regretted my decision, but it was too late. The damage was done. I got bullied anyway and the one person who could have been my friend through it all was now my enemy. High school sucked! Not only did the bullying intensify but I literally had no one in school who would be my friend. I would spend lunch hiding in the library because no one would sit with me in the cafeteria. It was the worst. And the threat of getting beat up only got more real because these kids were practically double my size. I couldn't wait to graduate.

Finally, my senior year came and about a month before graduation I found a note left on my car. It was from Philip. He said he needed to talk to me right away. I ignored the note.

Later that evening, while I was at home alone, I heard a knock at the door. It was Philip. He asked if he could come inside and talk to me. I let him in. We stood in the kitchen while he told me he had discovered he was gay. I asked, "You didn't know that?" He said he hadn't known until just then and was coming to tell me. He wanted to know if I was gay too. I thought about it and said, "No I'm not gay. I might be bi, but I'm not gay." He looked angry when I said that and responded, "Well, you'd better stay away from the rest areas on 195 because you're not going to like what you see." Then, without saying goodbye, he walked out of the house.

At that time, I was working at a movie theater in Seekonk. I had to drive by those rest areas he was talking about on my way to and from work. Intrigued by what he said, I stopped at one that night after work. I parked my car and waited. I saw other men parking their cars and some would get out of their cars and walk into the woods behind the rest area. They would be in there for some time and then walk back to their cars and drive off. Some would hover right along the edge of the woods and wait for others to walk in. I wondered what was going on in those woods. I didn't do anything that night or the next night, either. I just parked and observed. It was the third night that I finally got up the courage after watching a really hot guy walk into the woods. I had been working the late shift that night, so it was very dark. I walked into the woods. A strange man approached and without saying a word started to unzip my fly, took my dick out, and started to suck it until I came in his mouth.

After I came, I got scared. I quickly put my dick back in my pants, walked back to my car and raced home. Once I got home, I took a long hot shower, scrubbing myself to get every trace of that man off my body. I felt disgusted, violated, and horrified by what had happened. As a matter of fact, I was so horrified, I went back the next night and let it happen all over again.

I continued to visit the rest areas for several months. During that time, I changed jobs. I started working at the new Disney Store at the Emerald Square mall in North Attleborough. I had two openly gay managers and a crush on one of my fellow "cast members." His name was also David. One night I stayed late with one of the gay assistant managers. I asked him if he thought David was gay. To which he responded, "Are you gay?"

I froze. I wasn't ready to answer that question, but I couldn't hide my feelings anymore. I said, "I think so." That started the conversation. He asked if I went to any of the gay bars in Providence. I said, "No, I'm only eighteen." He mentioned a bar named Gerardo's. He said he and his partner would go there and frequently saw gay guys who looked underage. He didn't think they were very strict about carding people. He suggested I give it a try.

He didn't know the exact address of the club. He told me about the general area where it was located in downtown Providence. This was before Google Maps. I looked the club up in the phone book, found the exact address, and then looked at a paper map. Paper maps don't have addresses on them, so I had to drive around the neighborhood looking for Gerardo's. Unknown to me, some gay clubs had no signage. Some were in unmarked buildings, some in "warehouse districts" where all the buildings looked the same. It took me about a week of driving around downtown Providence to find it. When I finally found it, I was too exhausted to go in and decided to leave it for the weekend.

Finally, Friday night rolled around. I sat in my car in the parking lot afraid to go in. My fear was two-fold. One, I was under twenty-one without an ID, so what would happen if I got caught? The second was, it was a gay bar. I sat in my car until I was about to pee my pants. I got out, walked up to the door, and paid the cover charge. The guy at the door let me in. He didn't even ask for an ID. Once inside, I was elated. The lights, the music, the energy of the crowd—I felt like I'd found my tribe. I felt safe and comfortable in a way I'd never felt before. Immediately, I started making friends with other patrons. After that, I went back every night.

I started to wonder if I'd ever run into Philip. I felt bad about how I had treated him that summer between freshman and sophomore year. If I ever saw him again, I wanted to apologize. After about two months of clubbing, I saw him there staring at me from across the crowd of people. I noticed he was talking to my new friend, Matt. He looked the same as he did in high school. I stood there wondering if I should approach him but then he saw me and glared, and I decided to keep my distance for the moment.

"I know that guy you were talking to," I said to Matt later. "We went to high school together."

"I know."

"What did he say to you?"

"He wanted me to ask you if you were gay."

Oh snap! She got me.

Well, that was the last time I ever saw Philip at the club—or anywhere, for that matter. (Remember his name, though, because he comes back later in the story.)

The summer after I graduated from high school, I started preparing to go to college. I didn't want to go to college, but my family made me do so. Compromising with them, I agreed to attend a two-year college. My SAT scores were somewhere in the mid-700 range. Almost certainly, I had the lowest possible score. I was admitted to Dean Junior College in Franklin, Massachusetts. It was just far enough away for me to have a dorm room experience.

Unfortunately, that did not go well.

I didn't think bullying happened at college, but I was still nervous about going and making friends. Prior to the start of the semester, I hadn't done much drinking. Once or twice, my next-door neighbor and I had stolen some of his father's beer and had some fun, but that was it as far as me and alcohol were concerned. I hadn't started visiting the gay bars yet.

It wasn't until my first month of college that some girls on the third floor were having their boyfriends come down from New Hampshire to bring some beer and have a party. Surprisingly, I was invited. I went. I drank. In fact, I got so drunk I passed out. I woke up the next morning in someone else's bed, wondering where I was. No one else was in the room. I got out of bed, figured out I was still on the third floor and made my way to the stairs.

When I got to the second floor, a girl I didn't know said to me in a snarky voice, "Do you know you have make-up on your face?"

I was startled. "Um, make-up?"

"Yeah," she said. "Go look in the mirror."

I stepped into the second-floor bathroom and looked in the mirror. My face was covered with lipstick marks and "fag" was written across my forehead. I was humiliated. I ran down to the showers on the first floor and scrubbed every trace of lipstick off my face. Then I got dressed, drove home, and told my mother I was quitting college. No way was I going to pay to get treated like that. I mean, it's one thing when you're under eighteen and not paying for school, but now I had taken out student loans to pay for a college degree I didn't even want. I was not going to pay to get bullied. However, I was too embarrassed and ashamed of what had happened, to tell my mother the real reason I wanted to quit.

My family refused to let me quit. "Fine," I said, and stopped going to classes. By the end of the semester, I had failed all my classes.

Then they let me quit.

Shortly after leaving college, I got a full-time job waiting tables at a big Italian restaurant in Providence, Rhode Island. Since my mom was not happy about my leaving college, I moved out of her house and found a roommate. We rented an apartment on the east side of Providence.

However, this did not last long. I worked at a large restaurant with many other servers, some who were twice my age and had been waiting tables their entire working lives. I saw how miserable and unhappy they were, and frankly, I didn't want to end up like them. Sure, I didn't mind waiting tables as a short-term gig, but the prospect of it becoming a lifelong profession seemed miserable. Even though college was a bust, I started thinking I could give it another try. I signed up for a couple of night classes.

This time I enrolled at Bristol Community College in Fall River, Massachusetts. My plan was that, if I was able to successfully complete these two classes, I would enroll in more classes the next semester, eventually becoming full-time until I was able to earn enough credit to transfer to a four-year university. Since I was going back to college, I asked my mom if I could move back home. I explained it would just be temporary as I planned to "buckle-down" to get good grades and transfer out eventually to earn a bachelor's degree. She agreed and so I moved back into my mother's house in Swansea, Massachusetts.

By the time I made it to full-time enrollment at Bristol Community College I was well-known on campus. This go-round, I decided to do things a little differently. For one thing, I had come out of the closet and had attended several pride rallies, including several political demonstrations. Back then, going to pride events meant more than just getting drunk and buying cute earrings. Showing up to a pride parade was a political act. It required courage and commitment. It was also less of a party and more of a political rally. Don't get me wrong; the party started just after the parade. But during the parade, we were marching for our rights.

When I returned to the college campus, I came back with a greater sense of pride in knowing who I was and what I was willing to fight for by getting political on campus. I was loud and proud! Ready to fight anyone who was trying to put us back in the closet. Together with a few of my friends we chartered the school's first gay/straight student alliance. It was called "P.R.I.D.E.: Power, Respect, Integrity, Dignity, Equality." Suddenly my grades weren't so bad either. I was actually getting A's and B's for the first time in my life.

With newfound pride I was determined to make something of my life. When it came time to transfer to a four-year college I was accepted at the University of New Mexico. I left for Albuquerque at the end of spring semester.

It was the summer of 1995.

Professional Bully

After I graduated from UNM in the summer of 1998, I got my first job at Pier 1 Imports. That was the beginning of my retail career.

My first boss was a bitch (for lack of a better word). She reminded me of the bullies at school, except she didn't do a lot of name calling—although she did call me a fag once. I don't know if I had this thought or if it is something gleaned through hindsight, but I remember thinking something to the effect of, *Hmm, if I become the manager, then I can be the bully. And if I can be the bully, then I win.* I don't know if that makes any sense to you, but it sure made sense to me.

Maybe I thought that was how I could heal from being bullied. Whether it would be helpful or not, eventually I became the manager and, without consciously deciding to, I also became a bully.

For someone who never considered myself very competitive because I always hated sports, I found myself to be awfully competitive when it came to my retail business. I wanted to be recognized as the *best* manager. I wanted my store to be the *best* in the district. I wanted to have the *highest* sales. I wanted the *best* conversion scores. I wanted to be Number One.

This competitive drive made me a successful manager. I frequently won district contests and awards. I was easily promoted to higher volume stores. It happened again and again with whatever retail organization I was working for.

Except for my brief stint at Big Brothers Big Sisters, I was a highly driven retail store manager. This track record of success became my excuse to drive my assistants and my employees to do things "my way." I was relentless in my pursuit of winning. Driving people to be their *best*, demanding perfection and an unrealistic expectation of excellence from everyone who worked for me.

My last retail employer was Ralph Lauren. Having grown up wearing mostly Polo shirts, when I started working at Ralph Lauren, I felt that I had "made it." It was the pinnacle of my retail career. It was also the best retail employer I ever had. Make no mistake, Ralph Lauren is a fabulous employer. I worked with some of the most talented retail professionals in the industry. When I accepted the position with Ralph Lauren, it was as an assistant manager at the Las Vegas North Premium Outlet store. This was the first time I'd ever worked in a factory retail setting. Prior to that, I had only worked in full-retail stores. It was also the highest volume store I'd ever worked in. Things moved fast. Everyday felt like a Black Friday.

In my first year I learned a lot about working on the factory side of retail. I also learned a lot professionally as I grew from the experience of working with other high performing managers who were my peers. Peer-to-peer feedback was a big part of the culture at Ralph Lauren. We were not just encouraged but *expected* to provide our peers with feedback.

One of them sat me down in the office to give me some peer-to-peer feedback. His name was Kevin, one of the most beloved assistant managers among the staff. He was one of my favorite managers to work with. We had a great time together, our workdays often filled with laughter.

I was eager to hear the feedback he was going to share with me. He said to me (paraphrasing), "David, I know you're a nice guy, and you like to do the right thing, but most of the staff here thinks you're an asshole."

"Stunned" does not adequately describe how I was feeling after hearing his feedback. "Shocked" may be more accurate. I'm not sure I can think of one word to describe how I felt but I was definitely in disbelief. *How could most of the staff think I'm an asshole? Just look at my results*, I thought. Clearly, I was absolutely not an asshole.

The next day I sat down with John-Ryan, the store's acting general manager. I told him what Kevin had said and let him know I was struggling to believe it. This is how I recall our conversation taking place.

Me: I don't understand how these people think I'm an asshole. I'm not an asshole.

JR: Okay, that's your perception. What about *their* perceptions?

Me: They're wrong.

JR: How are other people's perceptions not as valid as yours?

Me: Huh?

JR: If other people perceive you as being an asshole, what makes their perceptions wrong and your perception right?

Me: I don't know. Because I'm not an asshole.

JR: Okay, so maybe you're not. But if other people perceive you that way, could it be possible that those other people's perceptions are just as valid as yours?

Me: So, you're saying that, even though I may not be an asshole, if other people perceive me that way, then to them I'm an asshole?

JR: Basically, yes.

What I learned from this conversation was that other people's perceptions matter just as much as mine, if not more, particularly when it comes to other people's perceptions of the kind of person I am. If I died tomorrow, it would be those other people's perceptions of who I am that would be all that's left of me. That will be my legacy. It lives in other people's perceptions.

Suddenly, what other people thought of me seemed very important. Not knowing how I could fix this, I decided to hire a professional coach.

I contacted the Landmark Education corporation. I had participated in their "curriculum for living" when I was in college in Albuquerque. I knew I needed some sort of shift, not only my thinking but also in my behavior. Working with the coach from Landmark helped me sort out some of the issues I had been struggling with since discovering the long-term impacts of having been bullied.

For one thing, I struggled when working as part of a team. Teams at work were always problematic for me. I couldn't figure out why, but maybe it had something to do with always being picked last. Professionally, when I found myself being a part of a team, I struggled to participate in a healthy, constructive way. My participation was usually "me-centered." I got *my* work done. I couldn't care less about the rest of the work, and if you had a problem with my participation, you'd better not mess with my work.

At the store where I was currently working, we were doing a *huge* volume, upwards of $50 million a year in sales. That kind of volume required teamwork among the management staff. There were about five assistant managers: men's, women's, HR, operations, and logistics. We needed to perform at the highest level, and I was most likely the broken cog on the machine.

My problem was that I was too driven. I followed company policy and procedure to the T and expected everyone else to do the same. Anyone who's ever worked in retail knows most company expectations are completely unrealistic. However, I made it happen and therefore expected everyone else, including my teammates, to do it *my way* because *my way* was the *company way*. This kind of arrogance made it difficult for people to challenge me because technically I was doing the job we were all supposed to be doing.

As a result, I didn't care about my fellow employees, their excuses or their lack of performance. Working with a professional coach, I was able to recognize this and begin to make adjustments to my behavior and tone. Some of it was as simple as asking people I worked with how their day was going; asking them what was going on at home; taking an interest in their needs and their desires and allowing them to do the level of work that was right for them.

These changes made a difference. By the time I was promoted to a general manager position in Seattle, Washington, I had converted most of the staff from perceiving me as an asshole.

My final week at the Las Vegas store, I received three going-away cakes from the staff and many handwritten cards letting me know what a difference I had made and how I was a role model for them professionally. I still have all those cards the staff wrote to me. They were some of the nicest cards I'd ever received in my life.

Unfortunately, once I arrived in Seattle and started managing my own store, all the lessons I learned were lost. As a new general manager who had previously been a high-performing assistant, I expected all my assistants to behave and work exactly in the same manner I had. It's a common pitfall, but one I was unaware of at the time. I demanded and drove my assistants to perform in unrealistic ways to produce extraordinary results.

When I started at the store it was still in its first year of operation. The store itself was considered a flagship location.

It was the first two-level factory outlet store. The company spent over half a million alone just on the store's art and creative appearance. The store was also struggling to meet its financial plan. That changed as soon as I got there.

Under my direction, the store not only started making plan; we were crushing it! Every month, my team of assistants and I made a bonus. Most months were *max* bonuses.

I want to say something else about that promotion.

When I arrived in Seattle, I felt like I had "made it." Truly, working for Ralph Lauren was the pinnacle of my retail career. I felt I couldn't go any higher than general manager at Ralph Lauren, even if it was just the factory outlet division. The truth is, that's where the real money was. Profit margins are significantly higher in factory level than full-retail, and the pay was higher too. After my divorce from Eric, my ex-husband, I put all my happiness into getting a certain job with a certain pay. I thought once I had both those things I'd finally be happy with my life.

And now I had both.

I was elated when I arrived in Seattle. I moved into my brand-new, mid-rise studio apartment at Pine+Minor. It was right on the edge of Capitol Hill overlooking downtown Seattle. Because the building overlooked the I-5 freeway, I had an unobstructed view of downtown. It was gorgeous. I wanted to celebrate my achievement, but there was no one in my life to celebrate my success with.

This was a feeling of loneliness I'd never experienced before. People say when you're down and out and no one is around to help, that must be loneliness. And it is; I experienced that later in my life. But it didn't compare to the loneliness I felt when I wanted to celebrate my success, and no one was there to share the joy.

If I had just turned around, I would have seen the reason no one was with me. It was because I had walked on the backs of every person who helped me get there.

The Appraisal

"I'll have the French dip." I gave my order to the waitress.

It was my first annual appraisal as general manager for the Ralph Lauren factory outlet store in Seattle. My regional director, Tracy, took Jamie, my district manager, and me to lunch to deliver my annual appraisal. It may have been my first year as a general manager with Ralph Lauren, but it certainly wasn't my first annual appraisal in retail. I'd worked in retail for over twenty years, ever since college, but my evaluations were always the same; no matter how hard I tried, my managers always found something to "ding," something to point out as a flaw. My goal every year was to receive no more dings. I'd written dozens of appraisals for my own assistants over the years, and I knew the protocol: Start with something they did well, then hit them with something they did wrong, and finish with what they did best. Then you give them something to work on in the coming year. That's how most appraisals in retail were delivered.

Until this one. After the waitress left the table, Tracy placed my appraisal in front of me. I was stunned! I couldn't believe my eyes. Every column was green. At Ralph Lauren the appraisal was color-coded: red meant poor performance, yellow meant opportunity areas, and green meant positive performance.

"Congratulations, David!" Tracy said, smiling at me. "By every performance metric, you've been a success! How does that make you feel?"

Tears welled up in my eyes. "I feel nothing," I replied. "These results mean nothing to me. I'm so unhappy." Then I burst into tears. People at the other tables turned to look at me.

When Jamie and I got back to my office, he slammed the door and said, "I can't *believe* you just cried in front of Tracy. Now what are you going to do?"

"I don't know," I replied. "Quit?"

"I think that's a good idea."

He agreed with me! I was stunned that he agreed with that statement. At the same time, I was relieved. Honestly, I didn't know what I was going to do. Obviously, my reaction to my appraisal was completely unexpected. If someone had told me beforehand that my review was going to be all positive, I would have been elated. It was the review I had always wanted, as long as I had worked in retail. It was the review I had always felt I deserved. I was a hard-driving, successful retail manager, and I finally received the credit I had always wanted.

But the truth was, I was miserable.

What was wrong with me? I had my dream job. I lived in a tastefully furnished, mid-rise studio right on the edge of downtown Seattle with an amazing skyline view. I had a brand-new car, and a closet full of designer clothes and accessories. Still, most days I cried while I was driving to work.

After my divorce three years 3 years before, I had based all my happiness into getting a general manager position with a six-figure salary. Once I had that and realized I still wasn't happy, I was even more miserable. I didn't know what I was going to do next, but staying in that job seemed unbearable. So, I told Jamie, if he could get me out of my two-year relocation contract, I would submit my two-week notice. He made a few phone calls, and by the next day I was released from my contract. That day I turned in my two weeks' notice and began to panic. *Now what?*

That night I called Philip, my old friend from high school who had relocated to Palm Springs. (More about our reconnecting online later.) Philip suggested I move there and try starting my life over. I told him I'd sleep on it and let him know the next day. That night I did some serious soul searching. What I really wanted was happiness, and Palm Springs seemed like the ideal place to find it. In essence, I was giving up on the straight world and trying to live a straight life in a gay body. I wanted to be free. I wanted to be myself and, more than anything, I just wanted to be happy.

I am a little embarrassed to admit it, but since I was nineteen, I'd had a burning desire to be in porn videos. Having just turned forty, I decided maybe I'd give it a shot. After all, it was now or never. My plan was, I'd move to Palm Springs, get into porn, and then figure out some side hustle to supplement my income. It sounded like a crazy idea, but it was the only idea I had. The next day I called my friend Philip and told him I was on my way.

But before I left Seattle there was one more thing I wanted to do.

Treasure Map

I decided I'd mark the occasion by getting a tattoo below the short-sleeved line. This was forbidden at Ralph Lauren and at most of the retailers I'd worked for previously. Tattoos were still seen as a career killer. Which was perfect, just what I needed to ensure I'd never go back. I wanted a tattoo of a treasure map on my left arm. The reason I wanted this design was because it seemed symbolic of where I was at; mid-life, mapping out a future I never imagined I'd ever see. Having just turned forty and being a gay man, would you believe me if I told you I never thought I'd live past forty?

It's true. In my early twenties, just after I had come out as a gay man, the AIDS crisis was in full swing. Watching the entire generation before me drop dead from AIDS didn't inspire much confidence that I'd live very long. I figured between the disco, drugs and sex, something would kill me before I turned forty. Yet here I was, totally unsure of what my future would be. It seemed like I needed a map.

As a kid I was a big fan of the movie *Goonies*. It's about a group of kids who find a treasure map in the attic, which leads them to an old pirate treasure buried off the Oregon coast and saves their neighborhood from becoming a golf course. I downloaded a copy of the map from the movie, as well as several other old treasure maps to use as inspiration for the design. I sketched out my idea for the tattoo to bring to the artist's studio.

I chose the artist who had done my most recent tattoo on my back. He was a local Seattle street artist who became famous for vandalizing corporate advertising with his "legendary" artwork. He was introduced to me by a local Seattle DJ that I had been hanging out with in the gay nightclub scene. I admired his work so much that I'd even gone to a few of his gallery shows and purchased several of his paintings. I loved his artistic expression and rebellious nature. He'd already done three tattoos on my back.

When I arrived at his studio, I showed him the inspiration photos and my sketch. I also had a few things I didn't want him to do regarding the design and placement of the tattoo. He asked if he could "free hand" the design on my arm with ink as opposed to drawing it first on tattoo paper. I agreed since this was how he did the last tattoo on my back.

Then while he was working, he asked me not to look.

Like an idiot, I agreed.

When he was done my heart sank. It wasn't anything like what I had asked for, and he did all the things I asked him *not* to do. It was too late. For one thing, I have a prominent vein going down the top of my bicep. I had asked him not to cover that vein; instead, he placed a mountain range right over the vein and drew a sea dragon going across it. I'd requested a simple "X" and showed him an example; instead he gave me an iron cross (a commonly used nazi symbol.) I'd asked him to give me a white flag; he made it black. He'd made other choices against my instructions, but these were the most egregious.

I was so stunned I didn't know what to do. So, I pretended I loved it, paid him, and left the studio. It was a long walk back through the Capitol Hill neighborhood to my apartment on the edge of downtown, holding back the tears. When I got home, I closed the door, sank to the floor and sobbed for hours. It occurred to me, lying on the floor of my apartment, that I had been bullied by the tattoo artist.

Of course! How could I be so stupid? Here I was, this big corporate retail employee of a Ralph Lauren factory outlet no less, throwing my money around at his shows, and living in one of the modern-style buildings he would have probably mocked. I represented everything he was against. It was no surprise I'd end up being one of his victims. Now the one secret I carried with me my entire life was laid bare in permanent ink on my arm for all to see.

My secret was that I had been endlessly and mercilessly bullied my entire life, starting in first grade and continuing through my first semester of college. Yet, I had never admitted it to anyone—not even my family. I kept it a secret because I was so ashamed. I never complained to my teachers about it because, frankly, they laughed at me right along with my classmates.

It's hard to describe the isolation I felt. I thought it was only happening to me. No one else got it the way I did. I was the one who got picked on every day, mercilessly. Taunted.

Teased. Pushed. Shoved. Spit on. Mocked. And of course, *always picked last for sports!*

I was that kid. And if you were too, we're not alone. Even if there's just one in every class, at every school, in every district, in every state, there must be millions of us. Millions who endured seemingly endless bullying by our classmates, teachers, school administrators, and if you went to Catholic school like I did, nuns and priests who joined in the chorus of haters, too! Millions who endured such abuse for so long.

Then what? What happens to all that fear, anger, anxiety, depression and rage after we graduate from high school? Where does it all go? They tell us, "It gets better," but it's taken me a long time to agree with that sentiment.

Since I went to Catholic school and we were often told about God, I felt God had forsaken me. Why was I being punished? When the school's motto was "Do unto others as you would have them do unto you," I certainly didn't see anyone else adhering to that Golden Rule. Which made me question the whole hypocrisy of religion, but that, my friends, is another story!

I truly believed that I was the only one. Certainly, everyone in my class knew. The teachers knew, which is why I never complained about it. I didn't tell my parents because I didn't want my mother to know her son was being called a faggot at school. I didn't even know what faggot meant back then, but I knew it had to be something awful. Possibly the *worst* thing anyone could be!

Nicer Things

After I quit my job at Ralph Lauren, I had to figure out what I was going to do next. I called my friend Philip from high school. (I told you to remember his name; well, here we are.) Remember when Facebook was new? When we were all excited about reconnecting with long lost friends and co-workers? It was that period of my Facebook usage, and I was married (well, technically I was a registered domestic partner) and living in Tucson with my other half.

It was the spring of 2010. About a year after I had created my Facebook profile, I received a friend request from someone who appeared to be a drag queen named Gloria Hole. I didn't know any drag queens at the time, so I refused the request. It came again. I refused it again. It came a third time. This time, Gloria Hole also sent me a message.

The message was something like, "Hey, David, it's me, Philip, from Swansea. Let's be friends again!" I was thrilled at the chance to finally apologize for how I treated him in high school. I immediately accepted the request and sent a message back, apologizing for how I had treated him back in high school. He seemed understanding and eager to reconnect.

He told me he was currently living in Palm Springs, California, and performing as a drag queen. By chance, my husband, Eric, and I had a planned trip to Palm Springs with another couple coming up in just two weeks.

Philip and I decided to get together for a drink at a bar in Palm Springs during the week Eric and I were there. It was late spring of 2010, which would have been our twentieth high school reunion. Philip and I met at a bar on Arenas Road, currently known as Quadz. Eric came along, too.

It was a pleasure to see Philip again.

As soon as we sat down at the bar, I went through my apology again. I felt it was important to say it in person. He graciously accepted and acted like it was no big deal. We reminisced about our job at the restaurant, playing Truth or Dare, and of course, coming out. The evening went very well, and I was so happy to have had the opportunity to apologize for something that had always been bothering me. Philip and I continued to stay in touch. After Eric and I divorced in 2012, I continued to visit Philip in Palm Springs on my own, making the trip from both Las Vegas and Seattle.

***

I was ready to pack my apartment and move to Palm Springs. I still hadn't told my family I'd quit my job. And that I was planning to do porn.

I'd decided to tell people that I'd been bullied, so I figured I had to start with my family first. I didn't know yet how I would come out publicly as being bullied, but I figured I had better start with my family first. After all, I'd never told them what was going on at school. It was always my secret. With so much to do to get ready, I decided I would tell them once I got on the road.

Here's how those conversations generally went:

Me: Hi, Mom. How are you doing?

Mom: Good. It sounds like you're in the car.

Me: Yeah, I am. I quit my job at Ralph Lauren and I'm moving to Palm Springs to do porn.

Mom: You what?

Me: I quit my job at Ralph Lauren and I'm moving to Palm Springs to do porn. I found an apartment there, and I already moved out of my studio in Seattle. I'm on my way to Palm Springs now."

Mom: *What!? Are you crazy!?* How could you quit your job?

Me: I also wanted to tell you I got bullied when I was kid. It started at St. Augustine's and went all the way through high school. It totally fucked up my life.

Mom: (unintelligible screaming)

Me: Hey, it sounds like I'm losing you in the car here. I'll call you when I get there. (hangs up)

When I got to Palm Springs, my friend Philip met me at my new apartment with another friend of his to help me unload my U-Haul truck. Initially he seemed excited to see me. However, that excitement wore off quickly as we unloaded the truck, and he saw more and more of my things. As we unloaded the truck, he began making snarky comments about all my "nice" things. When we were done unloading, I took him and his friend out to eat. His initial excitement to see me turned into a slow burning resentment. By the time we finished eating, I could tell he was not happy I was there.

We continued to hang out often and I would support him by attending all his drag shows. Over the course of about two years, I found myself apologizing repeatedly for what I had done when I was fifteen years old.

His insults and negative comments became overwhelming. The insults came to a crescendo when, at my apartment, he threw himself down on my patio set declaring, "*You always end up with nicer things!*" Slamming himself into the chaise he snapped the wooden support beam and broke the chair. I was stunned. Not only that, but he then proceeded to insult my "cheap" furniture and insinuate that I was trying to hurt him.

This was ridiculous.

First, I had bought that patio furniture with him in mind. We would always hang out at my place. I'd never even been inside Philip's apartment. He would always come over to my place. Since I had just a one-room studio, we would always end up sitting on my bed talking or just hanging out. My studio came with a large outdoor patio. Deciding to take advantage of this extra space, I thought it would be a good idea to buy a patio set. I looked for something that would look and feel like living room furniture. Philip was a big guy, and I wanted something that he would feel comfortable sitting in. I shopped on Amazon and read reviews. When I found a set within my price range and had good reviews for large people, I bought it. It was a solid wood, sectional sofa design with custom cushions. It looked like a rustic living room sectional, and it was very comfortable with generous size seating. For him to slam himself down like that, saying what he said at the same time, it all felt very intentional. As if he was almost trying to break it.

Which he did.

I was so shocked by the whole thing I didn't accuse him of anything at the time. I remember mentioning how I had "read the reviews" prior to buying the set. He left shortly after that incident.

After Philip left, I decided to call my boss, Kent. I asked him, if a friend of his came over to his house and broke something, would that person still be his friend? His response was simple: "Only if the friend apologized and offered to repair or replace it."

That was it! I decided Philip was no longer my friend since neither of those things happened. Plus, I was fed up with apologizing repeatedly for something I did when I was only fifteen. The next time Philip reached out to me, which was about a month after he broke my patio furniture, I told him I wanted an apology for what he had done. He refused. He continued to blame me for everything, and that was the last time I spoke to him.

Acting In Porn

My first couple years in Palm Springs were tough. I came here without any employment, trying to stretch $20,000 as long as I could until I found a job. I did manage in my first year here to shoot that porn I had been wanting to do since I was nineteen. Before I had left Seattle, I filled out applications online with all the gay porn studios I was interested in working with. I didn't get any responses.

Well, that's not true. One studio executive told me, "Don't quit your day job."

I thought, *Too late, bitch!*

I applied to one more studio, my last choice. They accepted me. One of the directors took to me and we started dating. During that time, I shot about a dozen porn scenes for them.

On the set of my last scene, I was questioning what I was doing. I was uncomfortable in the scene. Nothing crazy; just three tops fucking one bottom. I was one of the tops. This was not my first group scene. One of the things that surprised me about doing porn and working with other actors was that when there are multiple tops in a scene, all the tops compete to be the top of the tops. I found this behavior a real turn-off. *I'm not here to compete with other tops. I just want to fuck this guy's ass and get paid, okay?*

The bottom in this scene was also not really "my type." I had taken two 100mg Viagra, and I was struggling to get an erection. Fucking this bottom (or I should say, *competing* to fuck this bottom) with two other tops no longer seemed like fun. Suddenly it felt like "work." Then it hit me: Was this really the work I wanted to be doing?

The answer was a flat-out *no.*

I'd completely lost interest. Not only that, but I wanted to just walk off the set. However, my boyfriend was the director filming the scene. I could hardly walk off the scene; we would be going home together. So, I mustered up an erection and then faked an orgasm. It's known in the industry as an "internal cumshot." Because in porn if you're a man, you get paid to come. On a rare occasion, someone fucking someone may forget to pull out to cum for the camera. That's what I did, only I was acting. I "came" inside his ass, got paid, and when my boyfriend and I got back to his place, I broke up with him.

Just like that, it was over.

This was not the lifestyle I wanted in any way shape or form. Sure, I had a little fun shooting a few scenes, but the reality was, it was mostly just for fun, and not for a career. I fulfilled that burning desire I'd had for so many years, and in the end, I'm glad I did.

Escorting, though, is another story.

Hello, Tina!

Oh, did I mention how part of my plan doing porn was that I would escort using my porn name? Okay, maybe I forgot that part. I don't know if you're familiar with what "escorting" is, but it's basically legalized prostitution. This is how it works.

When you're a prostitute, people pay you to have sex with them. That's illegal in most places. When you're an escort, people pay you for "the time" it takes to have sex with you—usually about an hour.

See the difference? It's very subtle.

The problem I was having with it was that one client after another who was contacting me wanted me to use crystal meth with him. At the time, I wasn't actively using crystal meth.

Sure, I'd done it a handful of times prior, but it was always when I was away from home. My experience with the drug was that it was far too powerful. I never wanted to use it in the same city where I lived because it was so hard to put down.

The times I used it were few and far between. But now, I had repeated requests to use it where I was living, and since escorting was my only means of income, I eventually gave in.

About a week before my rent was due, I had a request from a client to use crystal meth. I told him I'd think about it. My response was that I would charge him double my normal fee, plus an additional "user fee" which altogether equaled my rent payment. My thinking was that he'd refuse such a large sum of money. He didn't. He agreed to the price, and I thought, *Oh, shit!*

I arrived at his place and knocked on the door. He answered the door from behind so I couldn't see him until he closed the door. The first thing he said to me was, "Did they see you?" I replied, "Who your neighbors?" He said, "No the people on the roof. Did they see you come in?" "There are no people on the roof" I replied. He insisted, "Yes there are and they're listening to us from the HVAC system." As he pointed to a vent on the wall. I should have known in that moment I was in trouble. This man was experiencing what is commonly referred to as "meth psychosis" It's where all meth users end up. Some get there quicker than others depending on whether you inject meth or smoke it. Since I had no idea what was going on I just rolled my eyes and asked him to take me to the bedroom so we could get started.

When his time was up, he wanted me to stay longer. He offered to pay me with meth to stay an extra hour since he only had enough cash to pay the agreed upon price. I stayed an extra hour and left with $800 cash (enough to pay my rent) and my own supply of crystal meth.

That began an 11-day run of using meth. Once I had my own supply in my own place I continued to get more, and more until I found myself on the 11th day sitting on the floor of my walk-in closet saying to myself, "hey David, you got a little problem here. You can't put this stuff down."

That incident began my addiction to crystal meth.

I can honestly say, I hated escorting. It was one of the worst experiences of my life. Not only because it brought crystal meth into my life, but it's also just the nature of the work. I did not enjoy bringing pleasure to other men who paid for it. I did not enjoy my body being used by others for money. *Ugh!* It wasn't worth it.

Actually, my body may have been worth it, but my soul was not. It was gut-wrenching work I found rather deplorable. I don't want to put down sex workers; I believe it has a place in society and the people who perform that work should be treated with the same respect as any other service industry. But It's dreadful work, and it's not for me. Obviously, I don't have to say, it didn't last long.

Laundry Zen

Finding work in Palm Springs is tough. I wasn't even looking for a high-level job. I just wanted a minimum wage job where I could relax and not experience all the pressure I had working as a retail manager. I was literally applying for the lowest level jobs at restaurants and hotels. I couldn't even get anyone to interview me.

I recall going into a bagel shop, applying for a dishwasher job. The owner looked at my resume and said, "Sorry, you're overqualified."

Frustrated from hearing that everywhere I went, I snapped back, "What are you talking about? I've never washed dishes before."

He handed me my resume and told me to go somewhere else. I was beginning to feel like age discrimination was a real thing. And the expression "You're overqualified" was just a nice way of saying, "You're too old."

While all that was going on, I started dating this young guy named Grant. He was the assistant manager at the newly opened gay men's resort, Santiago. Santiago had been recently purchased by new owners and completely remodeled. The general manager was a guy named J.M.

One night after giving Grant what I was sure to have been the best fuck of his life, I asked if he could get me an interview with J.M. I told him I was willing to do anything. The next week I had an interview with J.M.

When I met J.M., he told me he had done most of the organizing and planning during the remodel to get the resort reopened. He mentioned that the laundry room was the one area he hadn't been able to figure out. With my experience in management, he offered me the laundry room position and asked if I could "figure it out" for him.

I gladly accepted.

The next week I started on what became one of the most fulfilling jobs I've ever accepted. I loved working in the laundry room. I loved the challenges of figuring it out and relied heavily on my experience as a former Gap Inc. employee to create systems and standards that are still part of the operation today.

Working in the laundry was something I had never done before. When you have load after load of towels and bed linens to fold, it becomes very zen. I had a lot of time to reflect.

Mostly, I reflected on my professional career. After all, I had spent over twenty years working as a retail manager, and here I was in Palm Springs, running the laundry room of a small, gay men's resort. I thought to myself, *What did I do wrong to end up here?*

Shortly after starting, I deleted my LinkedIn profile. I remember thinking, *Gosh, if any of my former employees knew*

I was working here, boy, would they laugh. I figured they would think I got exactly what I deserved, and I did.

Getting shit out of sheets was not the most glamorous job, but the truth is, anyone who thought I deserved it was right. But the joke was on them, because this was the most rewarding job I ever worked at. I absolutely loved it.

Open Mic

I had time to reflect upon something else while working in the laundry room. Remember that tattoo I got before leaving Seattle? You know, the one that exposed me as someone who'd been bullied? I had come out to my family as someone who had been bullied, but that wasn't enough. I knew I needed to own up to that "publicly" in some way, but how?

My fear of people finding out was that, if they did, the bullying would start all over again. Telling people one at a time wasn't going to cut it; I had to make some kind of public announcement to really face my fear. But where and how?

While I was working in the laundry room, I came up with an idea. First, I started a blog. The blog was called, "The Diary of Gene." I made up a pen name for myself, Gene Defected. I didn't want to use my real name just in case things didn't go well. Reflections on the long-term consequences of having been bullied became the subject matter of the blog.

Then I had another idea.

I'd been trying to figure out a way I could confront my fear of people finding out I'd been bullied. I was already writing in my blog about the long-term consequences of being bullied. The idea came to me when I was thinking of ways that I could promote the blog: Where could I have a free platform to speak publicly? An open-mic night at a comedy club!

It sounded crazy, but I thought, *Why not?*

I didn't have any other ideas of how I'd confront my fear of people finding out. My thought process was that if I came up with some jokes about being bullied, I could at some point reveal to the audience that I had been bullied.

My fear was that if I revealed to an audience that I had been bullied, someone in the back of the crowd might yell something like, "Sit down, faggot!"

I needed to have a strategy to deal with any potential heckling. My first line of defense was to be so outrageous and offensive with my material that it would catch people off-guard. It started with my opening line, which went something like this: "Hi, I'm Gene Defected. I'm not defected like retarded, I'm just gay!" My other strategy involved how to handle being called a faggot.

First, let me just say, if you're one of those people who have a problem with me using the word "faggot," I've got news for you. I was called a faggot every day for the first twenty years of my life. I think I got the point!

Do you understand what I'm saying? I'm, like, the biggest faggot on earth.

I didn't even know I was a faggot until other kids said it.

Let me tell you something else: For all you straight people out there who don't like gay people, maybe stop calling us faggots all the time and there won't be so many of us. You see how that works?

I'll give you another example. When I was in the seventh grade, the other kids at school started calling me a "butt-buddy." I thought, *Oh, what the hell is this? I don't even know what a butt-buddy is.*

Then one day I'm on the bus going home from school. I mentioned that, when I was in school, I took the city bus. It was called the RIPTA bus (Rhode Island Public Transit Authority.) I used to sit in those front two rows that faced each other. I liked sitting right behind the driver. It felt safe and I liked being able to see who was about to get on the bus. Just in case one of my bullies was about to get on, I could get off. I was always looking for my exit strategy back then. I also found it mildly entertaining watching the bus driver interact with the other riders.

So, one day, I'm on the bus, sitting up front, and this young guy wearing tight, gray shorts gets on the bus. As he walks past me, I couldn't help noticing his big butt in those tight shorts. I watched that butt walk all the way to the back of the bus and sit down.

I immediately turned away so I wouldn't get caught, and I thought to myself, *maybe the kids at school are right, that guy's butt is going to be my new buddy!*

What can I say? I like big butts, and I cannot lie. You understand what I'm saying?

Let me tell you something else. When you're gay, you're born with a sixth sense. In the gay community it's referred to as "gaydar." It's this sixth sense we all have that lets us know who else is gay without having to say anything to each other. It's like we can just sense it.

So, here's how that works. Let's say you're walking down the street, and you see some guy. You don't know him from Adam, but you think, *Hey look at that faggot over there*, and you yell, "Hey, faggot!"

Well, guess what? You spot it, you got it! That's how that works. It takes one to know one.

Congratulations! You've got gaydar, which means you're gay too.

So be careful with that word. I'd hate for you to out yourself without even knowing it.

You straight people are the worst when it comes to calling people faggots. You love doing it behind our backs.

I used to work with a couple of straight guys. One day I was standing with our boss, Mike, and the other guy, Ralph, threw a roll of masking tape at us. Mike yelled at him, "Quit throwing shit, faggot."

Immediately he caught himself and said, "Oops, sorry."

I said, "It's okay. You wanna see how the gays do it?"

He said, "Yeah."

I threw the tape back at Ralph and said, "Gurrl, quit throwing shit!"

That's how the gays insult each other. Not that I'm putting down girls—or women, for that matter. My point is that the gays are no strangers to bullying each other. As a matter of fact, the gays are significantly better at bullying than straight people. This may sound strange and twisted but think about it for a second. Most of us gays were bullied as children, so naturally, wouldn't we take what straight people do and then do it better?

More about that later.

First, don't you want to know how my stand-up routine went? What happened when I revealed to the crowd that I had been bullied?

I revealed, "I'm that kid. I'm the one everyone bullied at school, and I'm here to tell you I survived!" The audience erupted into applause! Some people even stood.

I was relieved. I had faced my darkest fear. I had revealed my deepest secret, and all seemed well. Driving home from the show I was elated. However, there was one thing that I couldn't ignore. Although my fear of anyone finding out was gone, I still had all this anger to deal with. Just because people were happy that I had survived, and just because I was no longer afraid of anyone finding out, that didn't change the fact that I was still angry about it.

I was mad. I wanted to know why I had been hurt so badly when I was a child. Why was I treated this way?

The answer didn't come right away. I wasn't ready to let go of that anger. It had too much of a stranglehold on me to just let it go. I had to explore that anger, and what better way to take all that anger out on myself than to take a hit of crystal meth.

Call it a perfect storm. Call it what you want, but crystal was right around the corner.

Now c'mon, did you think that kid who got bullied all the time wasn't going to end up on drugs someday? Seriously, does anyone even think about what happens to us kids who got bullied? Do you ever wonder where we are now?

Probably not, because you didn't care about us when we were getting bullied, so why start now? The truth is, I don't care whether the bullies care. This is my life I'm talking about. My life and the lives of everyone else who got bullied are just as valuable and important as those who did the bullying.

Grow up!

What happens to us in elementary school shouldn't dictate our self-worth for the rest of our lives. But who am I to tell you what you should or shouldn't do? I'm telling you what I did, what worked for me to recover from that experience and take my life back.

The rest is up to you.

The Lohan Cycle

At this point you may be wondering, *How* did *you take your life back?*

Well, it started the day I came home from work, afraid to walk into an elementary school. The inquiry into how I would heal from the experience of having been bullied has been an almost twenty-year journey. Reflection. Therapy. Writing. Sharing. Practicing new behaviors. Facing my fears. And ultimately, breaking what I call the "Lohan Cycle" I was in. The cycle of being a victim to a group of bullies.

How I broke that cycle was, *I stopped playing their game.* That's what I learned.

If you want to beat someone at their own game, you stop playing their game.

Instead, you start playing your *own* game with your *own* set of rules. To do this, you first have to shut off communication with these individuals. Then you play by a new set of rules, which they won't know because you are no longer communicating with them. When they don't know the rules you're playing by, they will lose. That's how I broke the cycle, won over the heart of my community, and ultimately took my life back.

You can, too!

This is the part of my story I've been struggling to write. This is the part that hurts. This is the part of my life that caused me to go through the most pain, the most struggle, and eventually the most growth I've ever experienced in my life.

What I know about growth is that it's not easy. Change is hard.

We all love to talk about how much we want change, and how much we need change, but actually changing? That's something few are willing to do. It takes effort. It takes courage. It takes a willingness to be uncomfortable. Once you've been through enough pain you will change. Because the fear of the unknown becomes easier to manage when you've had enough of the pain and suffering of getting the same old results, over and over again.

And boy, have I suffered enough. That I can tell you, for sure.

I'm done with suffering. That is why this is the hardest part of my story for me to write. In many ways I just want to forget it all. Just let it go and move on. I don't want to be reminded of the hurt and the tears and the pain of my experience. Most of which happened just in the past four years. It's a barely healed wound, but it's healed.

I believe my experience may give hope to someone else who has been through a similar situation. Since I've already realized millions of us have been bullied, my story could be of value to one of them. Therefore, I will write this not just for those of us who were bullied, but for anyone who ever kicked me when I was down. I will write this for anyone who has tried to hold me back, and for anyone who has ever stalked, harassed, or bullied me online.

My story is for you!

Mean ~~Girls~~ Gays

Well, before I get into more recent events, I have to go back to when I first recognized this "Lohan Cycle" of behavior. It occurred when I was living in Las Vegas.

I was recently divorced and had begun making friends at social events. Soon I found myself hanging around with some of the A-list gays of Las Vegas. One night we were out at one of the gay bars off the strip. It was a large two-story club with a big dance floor on the first floor and a smaller intimate lounge upstairs. We were upstairs having a conversation at one of the bar tables.

Back then I smoked cigarettes socially, but because I was from the east coast, I was always looking for the "smoking section." I could not seem to adapt to the fact that in Vegas, you could smoke pretty much anywhere.

When I wanted to smoke, I would go looking for the smoking section. Which meant I would walk around the club until I saw someone smoking and think, *Ah, this must be the smoking section.* Then I'd light up and smoke a cigarette.

While hanging out with my friends one evening, I decided I wanted a cigarette. I let them know I was going to have a cigarette and stepped away from the group to go looking for the smoking area.

When I was done, I started walking back upstairs to rejoin my friends. When I got to the top of the stairs they caught my eye. I noticed all three of them were smoking. I don't know if they could see me, but it looked as if they were staring right at me, cigarette smoke hanging low around their eyes.

I paused and thought to myself, *Oh my god, they're smoking too! Why didn't they join me in the smoking area?* Then it hit me: *These are not my friends, yet they pretend to be my friends, but they must not be if they didn't want to have a cigarette with me or even tell me that I could have had a cigarette at the table.*

That's when I started to notice this weird vibe I was putting off. I can't describe it any other way than me being the Lohan to a bunch of mean girls, or as I call them, "mean gays."

Now before I get into the "what happened" in Palm Springs, I need to start with how I met some of the individuals involved.

First there was Philip, my old friend from high school. Obviously, things didn't go well between us. Based on how his other drag friends would react to me when I would go see his show, I got the feeling he wasn't saying anything nice about me behind my back.

That aside, it was when I went into rehab at the McIntyre House in L.A. that I met one of the individuals who attempted to destroy my reputation in Palm Springs. During the first year of my crystal meth use, I realized I had a problem. I started seeing a drug counselor shortly after realizing I was getting into trouble. It didn't take long for me to see this was going to be a hard habit to break.

At first, I tried to quit on my own. I thought, with some therapy and behavior modifications, I could get a handle on my addiction. Unfortunately, that's not how things worked out. After several failed attempts to stay clean I lost a bet with my drug counselor and ended up admitting myself to rehab. It was a year-long program.

It was there I met Adam Clinger. When I first met Adam, I was struck by his body and his looks. He looked like the man of my dreams.

What I mean by that is, when I first came out gay, I used to fantasize about my gay wedding. It was a summer wedding at the Breakers mansion in Newport, Rhode Island. My husband and I were in white tuxedos with madras bow ties. My husband in that dream was shorter and huskier than me, with dirty blonde hair.

When I met Adam, he looked just like that guy. But it was rehab, so of course, sex was against the rules. Honestly, sex was the last thing on my mind at rehab. Until it wasn't, and that's when I left.

However, Adam left earlier than me. He left the program after I'd been there about two months. When he left rehab, I thought I'd never see him again. I stayed in rehab for about five months. I went back after being out for two months and completed one more month. After six total months of rehab, I threw in the towel and decided to chart my own course for recovery.

I landed back in Palm Springs, making an earnest attempt to live my life and stay sober. I got a new apartment and managed to get my job back in the laundry room at Santiago. My sobriety didn't last long. I struggled to stay clean for more than thirty days at a time. That was the cycle I was in when, out on a relapse, I ran into Adam on a hook-up app called "Scruff."

He came over while we were both in a relapse. As we got caught up with each other's lives, he mentioned he'd had a crush on me when we were in rehab together. I was thrilled to hear that because I hadn't picked up on that energy when we were in rehab together. Out of rehab, he was struggling with homelessness, living out of his car. I let him know he could stay with me whenever he needed and was welcome to whatever I had in the house.

We had a good time together and slowly became good friends. We weren't just friends though; we were having sex as well. A lot of sex! He was at my apartment almost everyday jumping up and down on my dick. It got to the point where I'd say, "Knock it off already. You're gonna break it!"

We laughed a lot. That was what really attracted me to him. Our friendship was golden. At least, it was to me. When I got divorced, one of the things I told myself was that in my next relationship we would have to be friends first. I never felt like my ex-husband and I were really "friends." That became an important quality for me to look for in my next relationship. I seemed to have found it with Adam.

Not only were we sexually compatible, but we were good friends too. We could be in the middle of having the hottest sex and just bust out laughing about nothing and then go right back to having sex. It was blissful. Of course, it could have been the drugs. I don't know. Either way, everything felt right.

Until it didn't.

One day I confessed to him I was falling in love. I wanted him to be my boyfriend. He refused. He told me that Tina was the love of his life ("Tina" is what gay men call crystal meth) and that he didn't have room for anyone else.

I was crushed.

Was I reading him wrong? I thought he said that in rehab he'd had a crush on me.

I was sure he felt the same way I did. I mean, he was over at my place all the time, eating my food, wearing my clothes, and acting like he was my boyfriend. How could he not feel the same way I did? Was he just using me? (Don't answer that.) At the time, I was too afraid to know the truth.

Instead, against my better judgment, I agreed we could continue to hang out and be friends. That's when things started getting weird.

Soon I found out it wasn't just *my* cock he was jumping on. He was jumping on everyone's dick. Then I found out it was with everyone I knew.

I was hurt. I told him I couldn't do it anymore. I couldn't see him again. I wanted the key to my apartment back. I needed time to get over how he hurt me. He agreed and gave me my key back.

It didn't last long though. About five days later he started texting me again asking if we could hang out. I knew I wasn't ready. It had only been five days since I told him goodbye, but I wanted that ass.

Going against what I knew was the right thing to do, I let him back in. This time things were different. Because he knew I had strong feelings for him, he tried to control me by declining my sexual advances. He rejected me over and over.

Now we were rarely having sex, but he was still coming over almost every day. It was beginning to seem like he was just using me for a place to stay. By this time, he was renting a room out of my neighbor's place across the street. He was using me to "get out of the house" when things got tense between him and his roommate, Paul.

Paul and I were no strangers to each other. We had met and played together prior to Adam moving into his place, but we weren't really on speaking terms at the time Adam was living there. Adam's attempts to control me by rejecting having sex with me only made me want him more. I became determined to get that ass!

Things with Paul must not have been going well. I believed Adam when he told me Paul was about to kick him out. I suggested that we get a two-bedroom apartment together. I knew he had a sketchy rental history, so I offered to put him on the lease to help him establish himself. I figured it could be a steppingstone for him getting his own place the following year, or if things worked out maybe we'd continue to live together. Maybe he'd come to his senses and admit he was really in love with me. That was *crazy* talk! I'm the one who needed to admit he wasn't in love with me.

Here's the thing. His actions spoke louder than his words. Even though he'd say to me, "We're not boyfriends," over and over again, his actions told me a different story. He acted like my boyfriend in every sense of the word. Not only did he spend many nights at my place, eating, sleeping, and wearing my clothes, but he'd also express jealously every time I left the apartment including when I'd get home. He'd want to know where I'd been, who I was with, and what we did together. We were so connected we could finish each other's sentences.

I helped him in every way that I could. When his car got repossessed, I gave him my bike, which he lost. When he was broke, I gave him money and encouraged him to apply for Covid relief, even helping him fill out the forms online. Whatever he needed, I tried to give it to him.

And the more I helped the more resentful and angrier he became towards me.

When we finally moved into that apartment, he seemed angry the day we moved in. I asked him, if he was so upset about living together, why did he bother to move in with me? He replied, "Because I want to destroy your life."

When he said that, I totally blew it off. I remember thinking to myself, *Yeah, right. Good luck with that. I'm not going to let you destroy my life.*

Living with him turned out to be an experiment in self-torture. He made me miserable every day. Nothing I did could make things better for him. Nothing.

When we moved into that apartment, he still didn't have any money. I paid the whole security deposit; his first month's rent; and the next two months, I paid the full rent and utilities.

All the while, he was complaining about everything. The temperature in the apartment wasn't cool enough. When I asked him to stay out of my room, he didn't. He couldn't respect a single boundary I set with him. He couldn't respect one rule we made for that apartment. He did whatever he could to piss me off daily.

By the end of October, I decided I couldn't do this anymore. We had been using crystal meth together the entire time. By now, I could admit that he was just using me for the drugs and whatever else he could get from me. Then I remembered what he said about meth being his number one love. I thought that if I got rid of the meth, I'd get rid of him.

It was October 22, 2020, my first day of not using meth, and I got myself to bed early. Later that night, he woke me up at 4:14 a.m. Adam was standing over my bed naked, holding a meth pipe, telling me to wake up because he needed to ask me something.

I was extremely irritated at being woken up at that hour, but when Adam wanted attention, he had to have it. "What is your question?" I snarled from my bed.

He asked, "Did you ever have sex with my old roommate, Paul?"

I said, "That's your question? That's what you woke me up at 4:14 in the morning to ask me?"

He was spun in a jealous rage over whether I slept with Paul. Of course I'd had sex with Paul, maybe once or twice. What difference did that make? He had sex way more often with Paul than I had. We weren't boyfriends, so what difference did it make who I had sex with and when? He didn't like hearing all that and continued to berate me about my sexual partners for twenty minutes before stepping into my closet and asking me what clothes I liked best so he could steal them.

I was still in bed at this point, asking him repeatedly to "get out of my room and leave me alone." He then stepped out of my closet and said, "Well, I hope you don't want anything to eat tomorrow," and headed for the kitchen.

Shortly afterward, I could hear a ruckus in the kitchen and decided I should go see what was going on. When I walked into the kitchen, I caught him with a trash bag in his hand as he was pouring my food into the bag.

That was the breaking point. I'd had enough of his temper tantrums!

I snatched the bag out of his hand and pushed him away from the kitchen cabinet. I was yelling. He started to walk backwards towards the living room. I grabbed him from behind and threw him down on the couch. I held him down yelling at him until he agreed to "cut the shit!"

When he did, I got off him and went back to bed.

The next morning, I woke up at 9:00 a.m. I had to be at Santiago for work at ten. I went into the kitchen to make coffee. The first thing I noticed was that he had cleaned up the mess he'd made the previous night.

Then I took a shower, got dressed, poured a cup of coffee, and went out onto the patio to have a cigarette before work. While I was out there, Adam came out and asked me for a cigarette. I was walking on eggshells. I was afraid to do or say anything that was going to upset him again. I don't remember if we talked much at all. As I walked back into the house, I remember he called me a "pussy."

"Excuse me?" I replied.

He explained that I was a pussy for not following through on my threat the previous night. Apparently when I caught him throwing my food away, I'd told him, "I'm going to fucking kill you."

I continued walking towards the kitchen to put my coffee mug in the dishwasher. As I was placing the mug on the rack, I heard him say, "Hi Kent, it's Adam, David's roommate. I just want to let you know David's going to have a bad day today."

I turned around and saw Adam talking on the phone with my boss.

I said, "What do you think you're doing?"

He didn't respond. He hung up the phone and dialed 911. When the operator answered he said, "My boyfriend just beat me up." He continued to tell them he was in danger and needed the police to come. When he hung up, I said, "Are you crazy? You just called the police. Do you realize it's over now? It's *over* between us!"

Then I started to panic. This was insane. I hadn't even hit him. What was he going to tell the police? I quickly grabbed all my drugs and paraphernalia and threw them in one of my neighbor's trash cans. Then I called Kent and told him what had happened. Kent told me, "Write my number on your hand right now." I was in shock.

Then the police arrived. I hung up with Kent and greeted the officers with Adam. I hadn't written his number on my hand.

Two officers were at the scene. They spoke to Adam first. Then one of the officers approached me. This is how I recall the conversation going:

Officer: Hello, Mr. Remington. Mr. Clinger said you're his boyfriend.

Me: What? He said I was his boyfriend?

Officer: Yes. Did you hit him?

Me: I can't believe he said I was his boyfriend!

Officer: Did you hit Mr. Clinger?

Me: No. Did he say how long I've been his boyfriend?

Officer: He said you've been boyfriends for two years.

Me: I can't believe this. He has made it very clear to me that we are *not* boyfriends.

Officer: Would you like to tell me what happened last night?

After I explained my side of the story, the officers got together and conferred. When they came back, one of the officers said, “Okay, David, I want you to go pack a bag for two nights. I want you to get out of here for a couple of nights and let Mr. Clinger cool off.”

Then Adam raised his phone in the air and said, “I got it on video!”

“What?” I asked.

The officer then said, “David, why don’t you go pack that bag and we’ll watch this video he’s got.” I went back into the house and started packing an overnight bag.

While I was packing, I was wondering what the hell he had on video. I was thinking, *What is he going to show them, a video of us having sex?*

When I finished packing the bag, I went back out to meet with the cops. One of them asked me if I was aware of what was on that video. I said, “No, I have no idea what you’re talking about.” He then held up Adam’s phone and played the video for me.

What I didn’t tell you is that during those three months of living together, Adam was so jealous and distrustful of me, he decided to put a surveillance camera by the front door. It was aimed at the front door because he wanted to see who I was having over when he wasn’t there. I even helped him hang it.

Because it wasn't mine, I had no access to the footage, nor did I even know how it worked. I didn't care. I wasn't doing anything wrong or shady, and again, we were not boyfriends, so I didn't care if he saw who was coming and going.

However, I also forgot all about it. He remembered.

That night, after I'd pushed him away from the cabinets, he slowly started walking me into the frame of the camera.

When I watched the video, I was stunned. Wow, I looked violent! I was kind of impressed by my performance. It really looked like I was the bad guy, especially when I grabbed him from behind and told him I was "going to fucking kill you."

Of course, the video was edited to twenty-two seconds so that, even though it may have been recording the whole time, it only showed my reaction—which made me *look* like the aggressor.

But that didn't matter to the police. The officer said, "Now that we've seen this video, we have to arrest you." And just like that, I was placed in handcuffs and charged with misdemeanor domestic violence.

In the police car, I tried to explain everything to the officer. I told him I was defending myself. Adam had been throwing my food away. He had been harassing me for over twenty minutes. He'd awakened me at 4:00 a.m. He'd started it.

That didn't matter. Even though Adam had no bruises, no scratches, no marks of any kind on him, the video alone was enough to arrest me. This was my first time getting arrested.

When we got to the station for booking, the officer told me Adam was granted a seven-day restraining order against me, and I was not permitted back at the apartment until that expired. However, if he decided to, he was free to go down to the Indio courthouse and get the order extended to thirty days. I figured that would be unlikely since he didn't have a car and I was his ride everywhere. But at this point, I wasn't putting anything past him.

The officer said something else. He told me that if I did go back to that apartment and something else happened, my misdemeanor would turn into a felony just like that, and he snapped his finger. In other words, he said if I even looked at Adam the wrong way and he called the police, that's all it would take for me to get charged with a felony.

That was all the information I needed. No way was I going back to that apartment to live with him again. Not a chance! I wasn't going to give him that kind of power over me.

I was taken to Banning, where I sat in a small jail cell with nine other guys waiting to get a prison cell.

I was beside myself sitting in that jail cell. *How could this have happened?* Then I remembered what Adam said to me when we moved in together, how he wanted to destroy my life. What I had dismissed as nonsense three months earlier, I was now beginning to see as his achievement. He'd had me arrested. My first arrest for a crime I didn't even commit. How could I have allowed this to happen?

It was that ass. I wanted that ass, and I wanted it too much. That was my crime. That was the reason I was sitting in that cell.

Sitting there, I turned off whatever attraction I had to Adam. It was over. There was no way I was going back. I knew I had to get away from him, but how?

First, I had to get out of this jail cell. I was absolutely *not* going to prison. It was a Friday, and the guards said I wouldn't get in front of a judge until Tuesday, not a chance. It was also the end of the month; I already had my rent money sitting in the bank. How could I bail myself out? The guard pointed to a phone on the jail cell wall with various phone numbers for bail bondsmen. I called one.

Within 24 hours, I bailed myself out of jail. I was regretting not writing Kent's phone number on my hand. To be honest, I hadn't thought I was going to get arrested. It was my good fortune that another cell mate who was also from Palm Springs was getting released at the same time I was. His father was picking him up. I asked if they could give me a ride back. They agreed to do so.

On the ride back to Palm Springs, I turned my phone on. I had a couple messages from friends saying something like, "Hey, David, I need to talk to you about this video your roommate sent me."

I replied, "What video?" Then they each sent me a screen shot.

Adam sent that surveillance video he used to get me arrested to everyone I knew in Palm Springs. He sent it with a note warning everyone about what a violent psychopath I was, and how they all needed to be careful because I was hiding who I really was from them. I was completely floored when I saw those screenshots! So not only did he get me arrested, but he was also actively trying to destroy my reputation with everyone I knew, including my boss and my rental manager. It was clear: *He was trying to destroy my life.*

When I was dropped off in Palm Springs it was around 10:00 a.m. on Saturday. I still had to work so I took an Uber to Santiago. Once I got there, I told Kent everything that happened and let him know I couldn't go back to my apartment. He told me not to worry about anything; I could stay in his guest room until I found a new apartment.

Meanwhile, Kent sent another employee to my apartment to get my car keys and pick up that overnight bag I had packed. Starting Monday, I looked for an attorney and began planning how I was going to move out of that apartment.

The restraining order ended at 6:00 p.m. on Friday of that week. Six minutes after it expired, my phone rang. I could see it was Adam. I didn't answer. I was still at work in the laundry room.

He called a second time. I didn't answer. He left a voicemail asking me, "When are you coming back home?"

By this time, I had already retained an attorney who told me to not have any contact with Mr. Adam Clinger. I texted Adam a generic response, stating that I had retained an attorney and was advised not to communicate with him.

I had planned to move out on Saturday morning at 7:00 a.m. I rented a truck and asked a few friends to help me load it and take it to the storage facility. When I arrived at the apartment on Saturday morning, I called the Palm Springs Police Department and requested a "keeper of the peace." I had no intention of dealing with Mr. Clinger in any way.

When the two officers arrived, we knocked on the apartment door together. Adam answered the door, and the two officers took him to his bedroom and let him know he was to behave while I moved my belongings out of the apartment.

Meanwhile, I started packing my things. I've moved a lot in my days, but I have never packed an apartment full of stuff so quickly in my life. I managed to get everything out without incident. I dropped it off at a storage facility and went on to work. It took me about two weeks to find another apartment.

Maybe you're thinking, *Wow, sounds like that cost you a lot of money.*

It did.

Receipts

Adam's little stunt of calling 911 cost me and my family over $5,000 just in terms of cash receipts. That included attorney fees, moving truck and storage rental, a new apartment security deposit, and, of course, bail. But what price do you put on your reputation? What price do you put on pain and suffering? Those are things which, to me, are priceless. It's taken me four years to recover from his emotional abuse and gaslighting, not to mention getting my reputation back.

Plus, for me to be able to move out of that apartment, I had to forfeit any rights to the security deposit, which I gladly did. *If that was the only price* of getting away from Mr. Clinger.

By this point, I regretted not following the advice of my neighbor Kelly. Back when I was still living by myself in that studio, Kelly and I had become close friends. I remember one day, back when things were just starting to go south with Adam, I was having a bitch session with her about him. I was telling her how he wouldn't leave me alone and kept coming over.

Kelly: What did you say his name was?

Me: Adam Clinger.

Kelly: Oh my God, of course he can't let go. He's a fucking Clinger! Did you hear yourself? Did you hear what you just said to me?

Me: Oh shit!

Kelly was right. He couldn't let go.

Even after I moved out of that apartment and told him my attorney advised me to have no contact, he still kept texting and calling, asking for favors. "Could you pick me up from work?" "I'm sick; can you walk my dog?" "Can I borrow your ladder?" I did three favors for him. I did them because I already knew my attorney would be submitting our entire text message chain into evidence.

So, I told my attorney I would do up to three favors for Adam to prove that he wasn't afraid of me and that he was the one who kept coming back to me. I knew the text message chain would show that he'd initiated all those contacts, not me.

Meanwhile, with each favor I performed for him, he kept saying, "I owe you one." I got the feeling he was thinking that I was going to ask him to have sex. Not a chance *that* was going to happen! When I agreed to the last favor, I let him know that after I did it, I would be calling in my favor from him. He wanted to borrow my ladder to hang some curtains.

When I got to the old apartment (at the time he agreed upon) he opened the door wearing nothing but a towel around his waist. I was positive he thought I was going to ask him to have sex. He even told me he "just got out of the shower."

So, I hung the curtain rod myself because I just wanted to get the hell out of there. I didn't want to have to come back and pick up my ladder.

When I was done, I told him I wanted him to do a favor for me.

He said, "Sure, what is it?"

I replied, "Don't ever call or text me again."

He instantly went into a rage about how I couldn't let go and how I was so obsessed with him, that I was the one who couldn't stop texting, blah, blah, blah.

I grabbed my ladder and walked out of the apartment.

Proving he was the one who couldn't let go, by the time I made it back to my apartment he sent me the longest text message I have ever received. It was a fifteen-bullet-point text message, and the last bullet point read, "I'm not a religious guy, but I am going to pray tonight before I go to bed that, for once, you actually mean what you said, that you aren't going to respond to this, that you no longer care, and that you're over me. I cannot think of a greater gift." When I read that I laughed.

My first thought was, *Save your prayers. Done.* Then I thought about all the things I had given him: friendship, money, housing, food, sex, drugs, clothes, a bike—none of that meant anything to him. But never speaking to him again would be "the greatest gift" I could give him?

Let me tell you something: If that's the greatest gift I could ever give you, then please let me give that to you every day for the rest of your life! And just like that, I've been giving it to him every day since.

So, let's talk about that text message chain. First, Adam ended up leaving that apartment in late December of 2020 and moved out of state to Chicago, Illinois. (I found that out from a friend who saw his post on Facebook.) He ran away and left me to clean up the legal mess he created when he decided to involve the police in our relationship.

While he was enjoying his new life in Chicago, I had to prepare for a court trial. I totally intended for this to go to trial. I was prepared to fight for my innocence.

The prosecution offered three different plea deals, which all involved my pleading guilty to a lesser charge of misdemeanor battery. They had to change it from domestic violence because there was no way they could prove their case. With a domestic violence charge, the onus is placed on the victim to prove beyond a reasonable doubt that they feared for their life in the situation, which is the reason they called the police. They couldn't prove this because Adam waited five hours after the incident to call the police and remained in the apartment with me the whole time.

Additionally, Adam dodged the prosecutor's phone calls for almost an entire year, dragging my case out month after month.

Meanwhile, I refused to plead guilty to a crime I didn't commit. My attorney verified that I hadn't committed a crime. He said, "What you did is called 'equal force under the law.'" In other words, my "crazy" met his "crazy," and I defused the situation without anyone getting hurt.

At trial, I intended to prove Adam was the aggressor in that relationship. I use the word "relationship" because we were boyfriends. I didn't have to say that, though; he said it. The first line of the "victim's statement" in the official police report reads: "Adam Clinger states that David Remington, his boyfriend of two years . . ." So yes, we were boyfriends.

Unless, of course, he wants to admit he lied to the police.

I didn't lie. There are over 7,000 text messages between us covering a period of more than eight months. Among the thousands of text messages are many in which he declares to me that we are not boyfriends. The whole document is over 550 pages. It reads like a drugstore romance novel.

When I first read the entire document, I was disgusted with myself. My behavior was absolutely pathetic. Believe me, I want to blame the drugs, but I can't. *Pathetic* is the only word I can think of to describe my communication with him over the course of those eight months leading up to my arrest. It's no wonder I was arrested.

Oh, and his behavior: blackmail, threats, gaslighting. It's all there in black and white (plus a few X-rated photos). Yeah, it's quite a read.

Now, before I get into all the things I learned about myself reading those text messages, it's time to move on.

Mean ~~Girls~~ Gays, Part 2

The next person I met who also tried to destroy my character and reputation in Palm Springs was a drag queen. Let's just say her name is Frau DuLent.

I met Frau at a place called Shady Palms Clubhouse. It's where I was going after rehab for twelve-step recovery meetings. We met there and, at first, nothing really came of it other than being social. Then I relapsed. And perhaps Frau DuLent did too.

I need to explain something here. When I moved in with Adam, I knew I couldn't afford the full rent on my Santiago laundry room job. I decided I would go back to escorting again. Even though I hated the work, I was in my active addiction so oddly enough it seemed like a good idea.

I should mention something else. Back when I was still living in my studio apartment, Adam and I had gotten into an argument when he called me "sketchy." I remember he said something like, "Well, if you weren't so sketchy . . ."

I snapped back at him, "*I'm* sketchy!? *You're* the sketchy little bitch!" After that I asked him to leave my apartment for the night. After he left (and remember, I was high on crystal meth), I thought to myself, *I'll show him who's sketchy.*

You see, my porn name was Rex. I guess you could say I resurrected Rex as "Sketchy Rex." That night, I created a Twitter and a Just for Fans page for Sketchy Rex and began posting pictures and videos getting high.

By the time Adam and I moved in together, Sketchy Rex had built up quite a following. So, the idea of escorting using that name seemed to make sense. It turns out, what seems like a good idea under the influence of crystal meth isn't really a good idea. You're not going to believe how it turned out.

I had an ad on this site called "Rentmen." I received a request from a client. One of the things about escorting is that, although the client may know what you look like because, obviously, they've seen your pictures, as an escort, you *rarely* know who the client is or what they look like until they arrive.

This particular client requested I go to his place. I received the address, pulled up to his house, parked, knocked on the door, and who answered? None other than Ms. Frau DuLent herself. I was shocked! I couldn't believe she'd hired me.

I had never been to her house before, so I hadn't recognized the address. I pretended not to be as surprised as I was, but clearly, we knew each other. She invited me inside, into her bedroom. She had been smoking crystal meth too and offered me some from her bong. I took a hit. Porn was playing on the TV across from her bed. I gazed at the porn while she was talking about what we were going to do.

I had already used drugs with Adam Clinger, someone I met in rehab. Since things weren't going well with him, I'd decided that I would never use drugs with anyone I'd met in recovery, even if we were both out on a relapse. The reason became clear as I sat on her bed; all I could think about was Shady Palms Clubhouse.

I was thinking about our recovery and how both of us should be in that room instead of sitting there smoking meth and watching porn. I turned to Frau DuLent and said, "I'm sorry, I can't do this with you. I can't use with someone I know from the rooms, because all I'm thinking about is how we should both be in recovery." I didn't ask for any money. I just left.

Several months later, I ran into Frau DuLent again at the Shady Palms Clubhouse. We had both found our way back to recovery for a moment, at least. When we saw each other, it was as if nothing had happened.

Oh, wait; I forgot to tell you how the whole escorting thing worked out.

On the Rentmen site, clients are able to leave up to 4-star reviews of their escort. I didn't have any reviews until a client gave me a 1-star review. And that, my friends, is how my escorting career ended. After the 1-star review was posted, I shut my profile down and that was it.

Fortunately, just around that time, Adam finally received those Covid relief funds I had encouraged him to apply for. Because it took so long for him to get it, the back payments meant that the amount he received was over $14,000. He paid my half of the security deposit and the three months rent I had covered for him. It was about two weeks after he received that check that he had me arrested. I guess since he didn't need me to pay his way anymore, he conveniently got rid of me.

By this time, I had begun my painting career. I was still working at the Santiago and painting homes on the side. I had become known for a technique I use for color blocking; painting two or more colors side by side with razor sharp lines.

Frau DuLent asked me if I'd like to paint some lines at her house. I went back over to her place, and we discussed what she wanted me to do for her. Since she had a large following on social media, I told her I'd do the work for her inexpensively in exchange for some publicity. She agreed and I started working at her house.

I painted gold trim stripes in her living room and hallway. In her bedroom I designed a custom four-color stripe pattern that wrapped around her headboard and repeated in her master bath. When I was done with the work and she was expressing to me the utmost joy and satisfaction with my work, I said, "No problem! I can make poverty look like it needs a cover charge." We both laughed and everything seemed problem-free.

Although that may sound like an insult, it wasn't. That was me patting myself on the back for my good work. I meant no harm when I said it.

But think about it. How would you feel if someone said that to you? Well, when it came to that publicity, let's just say, no jobs came from it. Back then, Frau DuLent and I were developing a friendship. We started hanging out, and she even invited me to be part of her bowling team. So, when no jobs came of the work I'd done for her, I dismissed it at the time as, *I guess she doesn't have as much influence as she thinks she does.* No big deal.

However, I was getting what I would call "red flags" that maybe she wasn't really my friend. When I was in the bowling league, it was with two of her other friends, and I was getting the Lohan feeling again. I thought, *Maybe I'm hanging out with a group of mean gays, and I'm the Lohan.* Of course, I ignored many of those red flags because I wanted to be a part of the group. Since being arrested and still having to show up for court every month, and since getting arrested had a lot to do with not trusting my instincts, I was much keener to listen to them.

Then something happened that opened my eyes. One day Frau DuLent and I were going out to lunch. We went to a local sandwich shop in downtown Palm Springs. While there, we ran into an old boss of mine; he ended up joining us for lunch. After he left and went back to work, I remember sharing with Frau DuLent how much he meant to me, how he was an important part of my life and how much he had helped me.

Fast forward about a month later. I hadn't heard much from Frau DuLent after that lunch. Then I stopped in at my old boss's work just to say hello. That's when he told me how he and Frau DuLent were suddenly hanging out all the time, and "Oh, by the way here's an invitation to a Tupperware party at my house being hosted by none other than Ms. Frau DuLent herself."

This wasn't the first time Frau DuLent had started hanging out with someone she met through me. For a brief time in my first year living in Palm Springs I had a roommate. After I didn't get an apartment manager job at the place I had been living in, I decided to move out. I asked my new friend John if I could move to his place. John and I met at one of the bars on Arenas Rd and we used to hang out daily at Happy Hour. He lived right across from the bars on Arenas and let me move into his spare bedroom. John was a personal trainer, but he also acted in porn and helped me get into my first porn acting job. We only lived together a few months until I started dating the director who worked for the porn studio where I shot most of my scenes.

A few years after my porn career was over, I reached out to John. By this time, he owned his own personal training studio and I asked him if I could work out at his gym. His response was strange, he said something like, "well you know Frau DuLent works out here?" I responded, "So?" At that time Frau DuLent and I were hanging out. I knew she was training there, but what's the big deal? I thought we were friends. John continued, "well don't you think that would be awkward?" That's when a red flag went up for me. Obviously, it wasn't a problem for me but clearly she must have been saying things about me behind my back that would make my friend John uncomfortable. So, he said he'd look at his schedule and give me a call back.

The next day he called and told me that he didn't have any time slots for me. Now back then Frau DuLent and I were still friends, and I thought to myself, "if she wants to take John from me that's fine." I'm not that attached and my porn career was over. I decided I'd just join another gym. However, when I heard she was now hanging out with my old boss, that's when I knew I had to draw a line.

When I left his office and got back in my car, it hit me; *I see what's going on here. Frau DuLent is trying to isolate me and take away everyone who's important to me.* She was using all the information I was giving her under the guise of being my friend and using it against me. It suddenly seemed clear as day to me. I couldn't ignore it anymore. I stopped contacting her and I don't think we spoke again after that.

Immediately I wanted to tell my old boss what I suspected was really going on, that Frau DuLent wasn't genuine, that her friendship was a scam. But the truth was, I didn't have any proof. All I had was what my instinct was telling me. And if ignoring your instinct had ended up getting you arrested and put in jail, you'd probably listen carefully to it as well.

Also, I respected and admired my old boss. Who was I to tell anyone who they should or shouldn't be friends with? It was none of my business. I'd let other people have their own experience and decide for themselves.

Since I'd stopped having direct communication with her, I also stopped talking about her. Her name stopped coming out of my mouth, and when others mentioned her, I acted like I didn't know anything about her.

I did, however, go to that Tupperware party she hosted. It was held in the month of November and all purchases were guaranteed delivery by Christmas. I bought a children's Tupperware set for my cousin's son back in Massachusetts. He didn't receive it until Mid-February. *Just saying!*

Shady Palms

Things started getting weird at the clubhouse. Don't get me wrong; I was certainly not the most pleasant person to be around. Let me just say, I wasn't doing myself any favors. You remember the comment I made when Frau DuLent was thanking me for the painting work that I had done? I used to make comments like that all the time. Those backhanded, pat myself on the back type of comments that always seemed to insult someone.

But despite all that and not being the friendliest person there, people still seemed to respect me. Or maybe they were afraid of me; I don't know. This weird thing kept happening over and over. I would see people out and around town—maybe at the supermarket or a coffee shop—and they would have no problem giving me a big hug and a hello. Yet, when I saw these same people at the clubhouse, suddenly they weren't so friendly. I would sort of get the "cold shoulder." It was weird and a bit baffling. I would ask myself, *Why do these people seem happy to see me outside of the clubhouse, but in the clubhouse, they act like they don't even know me?* It almost felt as if, in the clubhouse, they were afraid to say hello to me. While staring at a picture of Frau DuLent on a poster advertising an upcoming holiday event she was hosting, I asked myself, *I wonder who they're afraid of?*

I had an idea. Since these meetings at the clubhouse were anonymous, I thought, *What difference does it make what name I use? After all, the whole program is anonymous.* So, I decided I would start introducing myself with famous female names.

Here's how it worked. Once the meeting started, we'd go around the room, each of us introducing ourselves. After each person said their name, everyone else in the room repeated the name back to them.

On the first day I decided to start using pseudonyms, I chose the name Mary Poppins. I sang the name to announce it to the room. Everyone was shocked. Maybe one or two people (out of about a hundred) repeated the name back. I continued to keep it going day after day. It was all Barbra, Cher, Judy, etc. And the reaction was the same; very few would repeat the name back to me. It was a noticeable difference from everyone else announcing their names.

Then one day I noticed Frau DuLent was attending the morning meeting. I hadn't seen her at a meeting since before the Tupperware party. So, I was surprised to see her there. She sat across the room, and I don't recall if we even said "hello" to each other; I don't think so.

On my drive to the meeting each day I would decide whose name I was going to use. On the day Frau DuLent showed up, I had decided to use "Madonna." When my turn came to announce my name, I said, "Madonna," and the whole room shouted "Madonna!" back to me. I was stunned to get such a loud response. I thought, *Wow they must really like Madonna.*

Then I saw Frau DuLent tilt her head to look at me. I caught her eye, and she gave me the most puzzled and annoyed look I'd ever seen on anyone. To be honest, I was quite surprised that they gave me that level of participation with her in the room. I thought to myself, *They must hate her even more than they hate me.* Each day I gave a false name after that, and she wasn't there, it went right back to virtually no one participating with me.

One day, I even said "Kermit the frog." Nothing.

Then it hit me. I thought, *I see what's going on here. She's the one they're all afraid of, and she's the one who's pulling the social strings around here. They just did that to show her up.*

At the end of the meeting, I gathered some of the books we used and started to put them away. Frau DuLent came up to me, snatched the books out of my hands, and said, "Goodbye!" very abruptly, almost as if she expected me to leave. I thought, *"Goodbye?" Hmm, I guess that means I won't see her again.* And sure enough, that was the last time I saw Frau DuLent at the clubhouse.

I was getting the feeling everyone was talking about me behind my back and, of course, no one was saying anything to me about it. Then I caught a break. I had been using the female names for about two weeks when I approached another member after the meeting. It was his birthday. Apparently, a group of members were supposed to be meeting to take him out to breakfast, but no one showed up. I said, "I'll take you out to breakfast." And the two of us went to breakfast.

Even though I had virtually no money, I still bought him his breakfast. This was the period in my life when I was actually homeless, living out of my car, and unable to get a stable job, so I made Uber deliveries. I was literally making just enough money each day to eat and put gas back in my car. On this day, I happened to have a few extra bucks, so I bought him breakfast for his birthday. The next day it paid off.

He pulled me aside after the meeting to let me know everyone was talking about me. They were saying that how I was introducing myself was disrespectful to the program we participated in.

At this program, we would agree at the end of each meeting to keep the contents of the meeting private. In other words, what you heard here, when you left here, it stayed here. So, if they were all standing around talking about what I said at the meeting, now tell me who's disrespecting the program? I had them by their spiritual balls and they didn't like it.

That wasn't enough for me. I was having a hard time finding a job. And what I mean by that is, my reputation seemed to precede me wherever I went. As a result, I was having a hard time finding work or being able to get a painting job. I was beginning to suspect that the individuals involved in destroying my reputation were recruiting members of the clubhouse to continue their lies in the form of gossip.

Again, I had no proof this was going on. All I knew was that I couldn't get work, seemingly no one would help me, and not only that; it seemed like no one was willing to even admit they knew me. I was becoming Palm Springs' Number One Social Pariah. Yet, I knew I had done nothing wrong to these people. I hadn't stolen anything—except maybe a few hearts. I hadn't broken anything—expect maybe a few egos—nor had I lied about anything I'd done to anyone.

However, that didn't stop me from getting really angry at the individuals who were believing the lies. I wasn't doing myself any favors, getting mad at the very people I was trying to win over. Still, I had to get to the bottom of what was going on. I read about a little trick the Kardashians use when they're trying to figure out who's spilling family secrets.

So, I went to my storage unit, and I dug out three old photos. Each one from a different period of my life. One was me and my ex-husband; one was me and my little brother, Matthew; and one was a picture of my first boyfriend. The trick was, you show one picture to one person and then wait and see what you hear. I brought in three pictures to the meeting. I showed each picture to three different people.

Sure enough, within a week, I heard back about two of the pictures from other people. So now I had two pieces of evidence that they were gossiping about me, but I'm one of those people who likes to do things in three. I needed to do the trick three times to prove it. Plus, even though they were talking about me, I still didn't have a sense of what their overall opinion of me was. I needed something to address what I felt all the gossip was about and how it was preventing me from finding work.

One of the board members of the clubhouse happened to be someone who mentioned that he helped small businesses get started. So, I asked him if we could meet for coffee, and if he wouldn't mind me picking his brain to help me get my painting business started. To be honest, he wasn't very helpful. He suggested I download and use an app to help me find painting bids. I downloaded the app and created a profile; however, I wasn't able to access any bids for work because my profile needed to have at least one review. Frustrated by seeing work opportunities and not being able to access them because none of my previous clients were on this app, I asked the individual who suggested it to me if he would be willing to write me a review. I mentioned that I knew I hadn't actually painted for him, but if he would be willing to just write something simple stating that he knew me and had seen pictures of my work, or knew any former clients of mine, it would be extremely helpful. His response (and again this is a board member from the clubhouse) was, "Sure, as long as I can be honest."

That was all I needed to hear. Now I knew what every member of the club thought about me and my work. I knew that if some sketchy, shady person asked me for a review, that's exactly what my response would be.

The picture was becoming clear. Not only did I suspect the ringleader, but it was clear she was also engaged in attempting to destroy my reputation. And to be honest, I wouldn't be surprised if she was in cahoots with Mr. Clinger. After all, when she was pretending to be my friend, it was the period when I still had court to attend, so I know I went over every detail of that arrest.

He was easy enough to find on Facebook. Again, the only proof I had of this taking place was based on my intuition and experience with others.

Take the Wheel

Something else was going on around this time. I was living in my car; I couldn't find work; and no one was willing to help me. I was delivering food for Uber Eats, barely making ends meet each day, and I was being followed and harassed by car gangs. (Yes, California has car gangs.)

Despite having one of the lowest SAT scores, for whatever reason my brain is actually good at remembering 2 things: Madonna song lyrics and license plate numbers. I don't know why; I just am. I was seeing a lot of the same numbers over and over, so much so that I started writing them down at stop lights. And sure enough, I was right. They were following me and doing things like driving in front of me at maybe ten to twenty miles per hour under the limit, sometimes two cars in front of me preventing me from changing lanes and passing.

Another incident happened when I was trying to sleep. I'd lived in Palm Springs for about eight years by this time, so I knew the streets pretty well. Because I was sleeping in my car, I tried to park on streets I knew were quiet and safe. One night I decided to park on Seven Lakes Drive. This street is very quiet at night. It's one of those streets in

Palm Springs that doesn't really go anywhere. It's more of a service road that wraps around the Parker Hotel. I parked my car along the backside of the hotel.

Back then, after I parked for the night, I would turn around and put the back seat down, then crawl from the front seat to the back. I didn't like to get out of the car because I was trying to be as discreet as possible. Similarly, when I got up in the morning, I would jump from the back seat into the front seat without having to get out of the car. I called it my "Dukes of Hazard" move.

I parked along the Parker Hotel, and I crawled into the backseat. As usual, I was meditating for about ten to fifteen minutes before going to sleep. While meditating, I heard car after car, driving by and revving their engines as they were passing by my car. It was very strange because I knew this was typically a very quiet street. After about an hour of listening to these cars going by, I decided to change locations.

Along Seven Lakes Drive, a side street cuts between the Parker and a residential community called Canyon Sands. I thought it would be unlikely for these cars to rev their engines along that road because it was more residential, and residents might be likely to report their activity. I hopped into the front seat and moved my car just a block down that side street. The traffic immediately stopped; no more cars revving their engines.

I was shaken. I started to cry. Who were these people? Why were they harassing me? How did they even know who I was? And more importantly, who put them onto me? Those were the questions in my head as I cried myself to sleep that night.

The next day I decided to park in the same place since I had felt safe the night before. The location was ideal because the east side of the Parker is lined with tall trees. These provide shade in the late afternoon. It was late spring when this was all happening, and the evenings were starting to get warm. Finding a shady spot was ideal because once you turned off your car, you needed to roll down the windows so the car wouldn't get too hot to sleep in.

I didn't have a current pair of prescription glasses, so it wasn't safe for me to drive at night. This meant I had to wrap up my Uber deliveries by sunset. After my last delivery, I would usually stop at the market to get something to eat and then find a parking place for the night. On the second night I parked there, I rolled down the windows and got comfortable in the back of my car. With the sunroof open and the back windows half rolled down, the temperature was just right. I got one of the most comfortable night's sleep I've ever had. I actually had quite a few good nights' sleep in my car. The first night I slept in the car I got the best night's sleep I'd ever had in my life. Well, technically not the first night.

The first night I slept in my car I was just testing it out. I'd already put in my thirty-day notice on my apartment and knew I'd be homeless after that. I guess this is where I should explain that I made the decision to make myself homeless in order to quit smoking meth. With relapse after relapse, I concluded that maybe my life was a little too comfortable. Maybe it was too easy for me to pick up meth each time. Perhaps if my life was a little more difficult, meth would no longer seem like a viable option. I believe I said something to myself like, *You're going to have to make yourself homeless to quit this shit.* I was high as a bird when I said that to myself, but regardless, I followed through. Once again, what seems like a good idea under the influence of crystal meth turns out to be not such a good idea.

So, I was about to be homeless, and I thought, since sleeping out of my car was an option, I would test it out. While I still had my apartment, I drove up to an area in Desert Hot Springs known as Worsley Road. It's a rural desert area, which at the time had been known as a local gay cruising area. Men would park off Worsley Road and walk around the desert looking for sex with other men. A lot of drug activity went on in this area as well.

On the night I decided to sleep in my car, I wasn't looking for drugs or sex. I was strictly there to see what it would be like to sleep in my car. That night didn't go so well. The area up in the desert is dark, with no streetlights of any kind; it's pitch black. It was also late November, so the evenings were cold, which meant less cruising activity. Which was fine with me. I didn't want to have sex; I just wanted to sleep in my car.

I put the seat down in the back. I'd brought a blanket and pillow from home. Not long after I laid down in the back of my car, I could see two lights moving towards me. I completely freaked out. I thought maybe they were a couple of aliens or who-knows-what in the middle of the desert. As the lights got closer to my car, I ducked under my blanket and hid. I was so scared I even peed a little. I must have fallen asleep because when I lifted the blanket it was morning.

That's when I realized the lights I saw must have been those little headlights you wear on your head. So, I thought, *Oh, I definitely need to get some of those, and maybe a box knife to keep in my car.* Just in case. You never know. The person wearing the head lamp had the Power.

I learned a couple of lessons on that first night. When I actually became homeless, it was a different experience. The first night I was facing homelessness and having to sleep out of my car for real, I was desperately driving around town, trying to figure some way out. I didn't want to sleep out of my car. I was scared of having to face the brutality of being homeless. In a last-ditch effort to save myself from having to sleep in my car, while I was driving, I decided to google "California homeless help."

The first response was "The State of California homeless helpline"; I dialed it from the Google search screen. This is how I remember the conversation going.

Helpline: Hi. This is the state of California homeless helpline. How can I help you?

Me: Hi. I'm a California resident. I was residing in Palm Springs, and I am currently experiencing homelessness. I was wondering what resources might be available to help me. I have no place to stay tonight.

Helpline: It sounds like you're calling from inside your car. Is that correct?

Me: Yes.

Helpline: Okay. Well, that is where you can stay tonight. Congratulations, and you're welcome. That's not going to cost you anything. And just so you know, this helpline is for people who are actually homeless. You still have your car, so technically, you're not homeless. But if you ever lose the car, give us a call back and we'll see what we can do for you.

Me: *What!?*

Helpline: Thank you for calling. (Hangs up.)

Now I knew I was screwed. I had to get used to sleeping in my car. I drove to Walmart and bought that headlamp, a box knife, and a few other supplies I thought would make sleeping in my car a little more comfortable. As darkness approached, I drove back up to Worsley Road and parked my car. This time, when I finally got in the back seat, I felt such a feeling of relief. It's hard to explain, but all that fear and anxiety about sleeping in my car and being homeless just disappeared.

Suddenly, I felt totally relaxed and at ease. I had no worries—no rent to pay, no job to think about. Just me in my car, alone in the desert. I got the best night's sleep I ever had in my life that first night.

The next morning, reality set in. Let me tell you something: Living out of your car may seem relaxing and carefree until you have to go to the bathroom. Then you have a problem!

I wish my only problem back then was going to the bathroom. I had a lot of problems, many of them following me around. I slept up at Worsley Road until it no longer felt safe, then I started finding places to park for the night on the streets in Palm Springs (which is legal by the way; I checked first). When I found a place I liked, I decided I would sleep there no more than three nights in a row. I didn't want to create a scene or become noticed. I tried to be as discreet as possible. I figured people wouldn't take too kindly to someone sleeping in their neighborhood.

What I noticed was that each night I parked, I would find other people sleeping in their cars near me. The last thing I wanted to do was create a situation where multiple people were sleeping in their cars on the same street. Since the location beside the Parker Hotel was ideal, I went back for a third night. That's when things got weird.

On the third night, after I parked and got into the back seat, I rolled the windows halfway down. As I was about to start fifteen minutes of meditation, I couldn't help hearing someone having a loud phone conversation. I ignored most of the dialogue during the meditation. However, after the fifteen minutes were over, I couldn't believe this conversation was still happening. It was beginning to get dark.

I looked behind me and noticed a shorter, slender man standing on the sidewalk about a block behind where I was parked, talking on his cell phone. I decided I was going to sit there quietly and listen.

The first thing I noticed was that this individual was repeating himself. He kept talking about drinking Diet Coke and eating salads, about losing weight. But he kept saying the same thing over and over. My thoughts ran in this direction: *Why is this person having a loud phone conversation on the street?* Then I thought, *Why isn't this person in their house having this conversation?* This led to, *Does this person even live in this neighborhood?* Then I wondered, *Is this even a real conversation?* That's when I told myself, *I want you to listen to this voice very carefully and see if you know who this person is.* I sat perfectly still, barely breathing, listening to the same sentences over and over.

Then it hit me. I knew this voice from Shady Palms Clubhouse. I knew who this was. Just as I looked back to get a better look and confirm what I was thinking, I saw this person's arm in the air just as a rock hit my car. A rush of anger came over me.

I threw myself into the front seat and started my engine. I told myself, *David, get out of here.* As I pulled out of the parking spot and headed toward 111, I began to see a convoy of cars and trucks pulling up behind me. He was not alone.

I was filled with anger and fear. I didn't know who was in the cars, but they must have been the ones who'd been following me and revving their engines the other night. Exasperated, I turned right onto 111.

As I made the turn, I said out loud, "I can't do this. Lord, take the wheel." That's when something unexpected happened. This is the part of my story that is the hardest to believe. I can't explain what happened other than some power greater than myself took over and drove us to safety. The only reason I know that is because if I were driving that car, I would have killed or injured several people that night.

In the car, I saw stars, swirling around me and the steering wheel. I do not recall driving or even having my hands on the wheel. I just kept one eye on the speedometer and the other on the cars behind us. The car did not go even one mile above the speed limit.

As we got out onto 111 and around the bend heading toward Farrell Road, I could see a line of cars behind us. I said, "Take us to Murray Canyon." I had slept there the week prior and felt safe. As we got closer to Murray Canyon Road, the cars behind us began to back down one by one. By the time we pulled onto Murray Canyon, the last car continued on down South Palm Canyon Drive. We parked on Murray Canyon, turned off the engine, and I wept.

I couldn't believe the display of cruelty I had just experienced. I was asking myself, *How could anyone be so cruel as to throw a rock at a homeless person's car while they are peacefully trying to sleep?* I thought, *As if being homeless and living out of my car isn't punishment enough for whatever these people perceive I did to them.*

The fact that they continued to kick me while I had already been down only motivated me more to stay strong and survive. I prayed to God for help that night as I once again cried myself to sleep. The next day, I decided it was no longer safe for me to sleep in Palm Springs. At night, I started driving out to the Whitewater rest area on interstate 10 eastbound. I would spend the night there. In the mornings I would drive back into the city and begin my day all over again. With nowhere to go and no one who would help, life was miserable.

No Talking

The only bright spots in my life were my meditation practice and a new manager at Santiago who offered me my laundry job back. I started meditating regularly around October 2022. I've heard it said, prayer is asking for help, and meditating is listening for the answer. I'd prayed *a lot* in my life, many, many times, but I wasn't so great at listening. I was one of those people who couldn't sit still for more than three seconds.

When I first tried meditating, I would attempt to do it on my own. What I mean by that is, I would sit still and try to breathe. I don't think I'd make it one full breath, in and out, before I'd throw in the towel and say, "Screw this, let's get high."

I needed help getting started so I looked on my phone for meditation apps. I started trying a few and had an "aha moment" while practicing with one of the guided meditations. The instructor wanted us to count our breaths. This was revolutionary! *I can count my breath?* I had no idea it could be so simple. Once I realized I could count my breath, then my competitive nature kicked in. That was the aha moment.

Now that I could count my breath, I had a baseline to compete with myself the next day. Once I was able to count three breaths, the next day I would want to count four, and so on and so on. I finally settled on an app I liked because it was the only app I could find that kept a score of how many minutes, days, and sessions I had completed.

The app was called 10% Happier, and let me tell you, after about forty-five days of using it, I was 100 percent happier! I was apprehensive at first about buying the app because it cost $99 for a one-year subscription. However, when I took an honest look at my spending habits, I realized that the weekend prior I had spent a hundred dollars on an eight-ball of crystal meth and a bottle of G, and most of that went down the toilet. So, it didn't seem so crazy to spend $99 on something I knew would ultimately benefit me, even if I didn't use it. So, I bought the app that weekend in October and I've been using it ever since.

At the intro to one of the meditation sessions, the instructor, Joseph Goldstein, mentioned that he had just gotten back from a ten-day silent meditation. I believe he said it was held at a monastery. I'd never been to a monastery, but I felt deep inside that this was something I needed to do. I knew my mouth was always getting me into trouble, so the idea of not talking for 10 days seemed challenging and exciting. I wanted to do it myself. But I wondered how. How would I not talk for ten days, living in the real world?

So, I decided on that day I would give it a try. I told myself, *Just try to not speak as much as possible.* In other words, don't engage in or initiate any conversations that day, and only speak if spoken to or asked a question.

I had to work in the laundry room that day. I told myself to avoid talking unless someone asked me something business-related. By the end of the day, I was struck by the results. By just keeping my mouth closed, every event, every work challenge—whatever it was—everything went my way. In other words, it was the opposite of how my day would typically go. Typically, I would try to convince and suggest and manipulate situations to go my way, and I was never successful at it. I'd always end up frustrated at the end of the day because things never went my way. Now I could see that by keeping my mouth shut, everything went the way I would have wanted it to go. I knew this was something I needed to continue.

The next day I woke up determined to keep it going. I was still just trying to keep my conversation as minimal as possible. Only speaking when spoken to. At the time, I was still smoking cigarettes so I decided instead of smoking at the break table, I would walk off-property to have a cigarette. I was looking for ways to avoid people and, of course, at work, if someone was at the break table, it was just a matter of time before someone else would arrive. I didn't want to appear like I was being rude by not talking. Instead, I thought, I'd just go take a walk.

It was the second day of the no-talking commitment, and I will admit, it was getting challenging. The first day was easier because it was simply one day, and I did it. The second day, I was already seeing so many things and having so many insights. I wanted to talk to someone about what I was noticing, but, of course, it was a no-talking meditation so I had to keep it all to myself. That was the hard part.

We are creatures of communication. Talking is our primary means of communication. However, in the absence of conversation, I was noticing all the other ways we communicate: body language, eye contact, symbolism, etc. It's like they say, when you lose one of your senses (eyesight, hearing, etc.), your other senses (smell, touch, etc.) become heightened. That's what I was experiencing when it came to communicating.

So, I went for a walk to have a cigarette. The Santiago resort is located just one block south of the Tahquitz River. Along the river is the Tahquitz River Park. I decided to walk out to East Palm Canyon Drive and go back along the river park. As I was walking over the bridge on East Palm Canyon Drive, I stopped to admire the view of the river park facing east. Three large black crows flew overhead. One landed in a tree across from me and the other two landed on the ground beneath the tree. This caught my eye.

Not just the number of the birds—three—but also the formation—a triangle. I was brought up to believe that the number three is something of a spiritual number. It represents the Father, the Son, and the Holy Spirit. When I tell you I was struck by the birds, I mean, it felt like they were calling to me. I'm not saying I was talking to the birds. What I'm saying is that they started the conversation. They seemed to be saying to me, "Follow us."

So, I did. I got off the bridge on the north side of the river and started on the path along North Riverside Drive. The birds took off flying, heading east along the riverbed towards the foot bridge at Camino Real. I quickly headed toward the foot bridge, sometimes losing the birds from my view. When that happened, I suddenly noticed smaller birds, hummingbirds and finches, in the trees seemingly guiding me towards the footbridge.

It was every Snow White fantasy I'd ever had. The birds were all gathered together guiding me towards something. When I got to the footbridge, I saw the three crows again. One had landed on the south side of the river path, while the other two remained in flight circling overhead. I quickly walked across the foot bridge and began huffing it up South Riverside Drive towards the bird.

While I was walking, the other two birds flew from behind me right over my head and landed about twenty feet in front of me. I stopped and looked at the two birds who had just landed. One of them caught my eye. He was the closest to me. He then started walking towards me. I watched him walk and it was as if he was saying to me, "Walk like this." In my head I said, "Ah, I get it. Slow my stroll."

So, I started walking like the bird, slowly and carefully putting my feet on the ground. Walking like the bird. Then the three birds took off and flew into an empty parking lot behind a church at the corner of South Riverside Drive and Random Road. I kept walking like the bird and entered the empty parking lot. The end of the parking lot was rimmed by a fence covered in shrubs. In front of the fence sat a rock where one of the birds was perched.

Suddenly, all three took off south into the trees behind the fence. I got the feeling they wanted me to sit on that rock. I proceeded slowly and quietly walked towards the rock. When I got to it, I sat down.

That's when I noticed the shrubs in front of me. Looking through those shrubs, I could see the Santiago break table. The birds had brought me right to the back of the resort. I didn't even know this area existed. I had never been back here before, but from that rock, I could see and hear everything that was going on behind my back. And because I had so carefully approached the area, they didn't know I was there. I sat there for a few minutes and decided I'd seen enough.

When I got back to the resort, I walked into the office, and told my manager there was something I needed to tell him. He was busy, so he agreed to visit me in the laundry room when he had a moment.

When I walked back into the laundry room, I had a confrontation with myself. In my head, I was screaming at myself for what I had done. I was saying to myself, *I can't believe you spoke! How could you say something? If you tell him what you saw, you will ruin it. I thought you were doing this no-talking meditation? Aren't you sick of ruining everything you've ever had? Don't you want to try to do this and see what happens?* The answer was, "Yes."

I remembered hearing once in recovery that we are only as sick as our secrets. Suddenly it seemed like this ten-day no-talking meditation was becoming a secret and, if I really wanted to be successful at it, I was going to have to tell other people. That's when I had an idea to save myself.

My boss walked into the room and asked, "What was it you wanted to tell me?"

I replied, "I'm doing a ten-day no-talking meditation, and I need your help."

He was baffled and asked, "What are you talking about?"

I explained it was an exercise I was doing for my recovery, and I just needed help letting the staff know that I was not going to be talking for ten days. Of course it was work, so I'd still need to talk about work when necessary, but I asked if he could please ask them not to engage me in any personal conversation. I told him I would really appreciate it. I further explained that it was only for ten days and that I was on day number two.

He said he understood and agreed to help. And that's when things really started to get hard.

I realized that if I was going to do this successfully in the real world, I would need to make up some rules for how I would participate in the ten-day no-talking challenge. Here are the rules I made for myself:

1. No drive thru. Meals would have to be purchased at the supermarket using the self-checkout. If I had to have take-out, I would have to go inside to the counter and wait until the cashier asked for my order.

2. Avoid eye-contact. In public I was to be as discreet as possible. Avoiding not only eye contact but looking at people in general. I tried to keep my gaze down and look where I was going, not at whoever was around me.
3. No singing or humming of any kind. Singing is basically talking with music. The idea was to keep quiet as much as possible.
4. In public only speak if someone asked me a question. And I was to *only* answer the question. No additional commentary; just the answer.
5. Work exceptions. Obviously, I was working full-time in the laundry room at the Santiago and therefore would have to discuss operations as needed, and it was to be operations only.

The next group of people I needed to talk to were the guys down at Shady Palms Clubhouse. The next morning, Day Three, I decided I would make an announcement at the morning meeting.

I was about to tell these guys that I would not be talking for ten days and, as a result, was letting them know to please not engage me in conversation or ask me to lead a meeting or whatever.

At the time, they weren't doing any of that anyway. I attended the 7:00 a.m. meeting at the clubhouse. Typically, I'd like to get there with the early risers. I would usually show up at the clubhouse around 6:30 a.m. If you've ever been to Palm Springs, you know that in the early morning, it's very quiet. This is not a big city. At 6:30 in the morning you can hear a pin drop. I'd arrive at the clubhouse, park my car, and start walking up to the clubhouse. The lights would be on, the door would be propped open, and I could see everyone sitting inside. And again, it's Palm Springs, so you could hear a pin drop.

The second I'd step foot into the door, all of a sudden, it was a big commotion. Everybody's talking to everybody, nobody even notices me walking in the door. It was so obvious nobody welcomed me there.

So, there I was, going into the meeting on Day Three of my no-talking meditation. At the end of the meeting, I made the announcement. It went something like this: "I just want to let you guys know I'm doing a ten-day no-talking meditation. So please don't ask me to lead any meetings, do any readings, make any announcements, or talk to me for the next ten days."

Now I thought these guys were going to crack up laughing when I said that because, look, they weren't doing any of those things anyway. It seemed like a concerted effort to keep my voice out of that meeting.

So again, I thought they were all going to laugh. That's not what happened. Instead, after I made that announcement, it was dead silent. The guy sitting next to me leaned in and whispered, "Thank you," in my ear.

I wanted to shout back, "You're welcome!" But it was a no-talking meditation.

I made an agreement with myself that I would only speak to make the announcement. Nothing more. So yeah, I was pissed, but I couldn't say anything. That was tough.

This was definitely not an easy commitment. But I was quickly seeing how my mouth was my greatest liability. And the more I kept it shut, the more I was learning. It was awesome those first few days. Not only was my ability to perceive other forms of communication deepened, but I was closely observing how others were reacting to my silence. People who were typically very hurtful towards me were suddenly kind. These were the people I considered the closest to me. The people whom I seemingly cared for the most in my life were no longer hurting me in the way they used to when I was talking.

Then it hit me: I was the cause of them hurting me. Whatever I was saying to them caused the hurt. Now that I was silent, I was no longer giving them a reason to hurt me. Suddenly I could see I was my own worst enemy. Not only that, but my mouth was the cause of all my problems.

Here's what I was realizing. The bullying doesn't end in the schoolyard. Sure, as adults we're not all calling each other "faggots" to our faces, but we find new "socially acceptable" ways to insult each other. Maybe it's being passive-aggressive. Maybe it's some back-handed compliments. Maybe it's "making a joke," which is just an insult in disguise. Maybe it's all those things. I was a master at insulting people without even realizing I was doing it.

Every word that came out of my mouth was an insult to someone somewhere. It never failed. All I could do was insult people. I mean, after all, I was bullied throughout my entire adolescence and teen years. I really didn't know how else to treat people, other than insulting them. Show me how to not insult people and I'll do it. Otherwise, that's all I ever knew. Insults. It was ingrained in my ethos.

The truth is, I don't want to insult people. I want to love people. Every day of not talking, I was beginning to see how I could love people more and insult them less.

One of the hardest rules I made for the no-talking meditation was no singing. I loved singing at work. In the laundry room at Santiago I would play music, sing along, dance, have a grand ol' time. Certainly, when I first started in the laundry room, no music was playing. It was silent and I used that time to reflect.

Once I was done dealing with a lot of the issues that brought me to the laundry room, I started playing music and having fun. This is also probably another reason many of my co-workers didn't really like me. Not only did I do an excellent job working in that laundry room, going way above the expectations set for everyone else, I was singing and dancing the whole time. While most of the other employees hated their job, I was one employee who not only enjoyed my job, but I could do it better than anyone else, singing and dancing at the same time. Totally annoying!

But hey, I didn't care. I was having fun. So yeah, not being able to sing in the laundry room was really hard. Music is an escape for me. I can listen to a Madonna song over and over and be taken away to another place and time. That's what I love about Madonna's songs. She tells a romantic story and completely takes me away from whatever pain I'm feeling in the moment.

During my no-talking meditation, I decided it would be best if I turned off the music, since it would be too easy to start singing. By the sixth day I got this idea to search iTunes to see if they had those old Disney storybook albums I used to listen to when I was a child. I thought it would be fun to replay some of those soundtracks I hadn't listened to since I was a child. Oddly enough, I was able to find some of my favorites: Mary Poppins, Cinderella, and even Jungle Book. *Perfect*, I thought. *Let's go grab the dirty pool towels out by the pool and then settle into the laundry room for a long folding session.* I went out by the pool to grab the towels. It was a Friday, late afternoon, and the pool was hopping as usual. I don't know if you've ever been to Santiago, but it happens to be one of the most popular resorts for gay men in Palm Springs, and this particular Friday was no exception. The pool was packed.

I got back to the laundry room and decided to listen to Mary Poppins first. I don't know why; it just seemed like work-appropriate music. I also reminded myself I could not sing along, and if I opened my mouth the music would get turned off immediately. I can be pretty strict with myself when I need to be. I had several loads of sheets to fold.

I started to play the soundtrack, and it was wonderful. I was having a blast. Even though I couldn't sing there was nothing holding me back from dancing. I was working out some amazing choreography folding sheets while listening to Mary Poppins. I listened to the whole soundtrack from beginning to end.

Next, I decided I'd listen to Cinderella.

Before we get into the soundtrack, I want to remind you Cinderella was my *favorite* storybook as a child, and for whatever reason, I hadn't listened to it since I was probably eight or nine years old. Even through all the Disney re-releases from the vault, for some reason, I always managed to avoid Cinderella. I don't know why because it was my favorite.

So, I was excited to listen to it again as an adult. I pressed Play on my iPhone and the soundtrack began with the overture. As soon as the strings came in and the haunting chorus of vocals singing, "Cinderella," a flush of emotion welled up from my belly. It began rushing to my face as I felt tears sliding down my cheeks.

Suddenly, all the pain and hurt of my childhood came to the surface. I couldn't hold it back. I dropped the sheet I was about to fold and held my hands to my face. I started to weep. My knees buckled under the weight of the emotion I was feeling. I fell to the floor sobbing. It was all the pain of my childhood. The hurt. The agony. The sheer loneliness I had felt as a little boy. Images from the schoolyard flooded my memory. The isolation. The fear. By now I was crying uncontrollably.

Then I noticed the laundry room door was open. While still on the floor, I lunged at the door, slamming it shut. Slowly I crawled to the back corner of the laundry room, sobbing and crying. Tears were streaming down my face. I grabbed a washcloth from the bin to wipe tears. The music was still playing. Images from my childhood raced through my mind. I was hunched over on the floor as tears fell from my face.

Then I noticed blood on the floor; I had given myself a bloody nose from crying so hard. When I saw the blood, I screamed. It was as if I'd seen a monster. Now I was screaming and crying. It felt like I was in a horror movie. Screaming at the ghosts from my past. All the tears, the sadness, the anger I felt as a child were finally being set free. As each song from the soundtrack continued to play—the overture, the stepsisters' singing lesson, and The King's Plan—I wondered when it would end. No one knocked on the door to check on me. I felt as alone and isolated as I did as a child.

At some point I realized no one was coming to save me. No prince was coming to pick me up. No one was going to hug me, kiss me, and tell me everything was going to be okay. I realized, if I wanted to get up off the floor, I was going to have to do it myself. Slowly I wrapped my arms around my body and held myself tight. My tears began to dry. I started saying to myself over and over, "Everything *is* going to be okay."

Just around that time the soundtrack started playing the mouse work song. That's my favorite song on the soundtrack and I was starting to feel a little better. My tears had dried. My nose stopped bleeding. I started to feel a sense of calm. That's when I got off the floor and began folding again. I picked up the sheet I had dropped on the table, this time imagining I was playing along with Cinderella's animal friends, folding in time with the music.

Then something hit me. I realized I was no longer hurt. It was as if the earth moved under my feet and I was no longer hurt by the world. Everything suddenly looked different. I stopped the music. I listened to the silence. I reached for my glasses. I wanted to see what this new world looked like, the world where I was no longer hurt by people.

It was time for a break. I had a new world to explore. I decided I'd grab a cup of hot tea from the hotel's cantina. I put my glasses on, grabbed my mug, and headed for the cantina located out by the pool. I opened the laundry room door and headed back out to the pool area. When I opened the door, everyone was gone. All the guests I had just seen lounging and playing in the pool had disappeared. The once-hopping pool area looked like a ghost town. I went to the office to find the manager, but he was missing. No one was there.

Oh shit, they must have heard me, I thought. Then I smiled. I didn't care. I wasn't hurt anymore. No one could hurt me. I got my tea and went back to the laundry room. I worked in silence. I no longer needed an escape from my pain because the pain was gone. I was no longer hurt by having been bullied. I had released all the pain from my childhood listening to the *Cinderella* soundtrack.

What started as an almost twenty-year journey was finally complete. I was healed. I worked the rest of my shift with a feeling of peace and serenity I had never known before.

Now, if only I could tell someone. I still had four days left to go.

The remaining four days of that ten-day no-talking meditation were the toughest. I wanted so much to tell someone—*Heck, to tell everyone*—what I'd learned by not talking for ten days. It was truly an extraordinary experience. It was one of the hardest things I've ever done, and it gave me a second chance to live my life.

Once I could see that I was the cause of all my problems, I could decide to make changes to how I communicated with people. That ultimately would give me a second chance at life. During those ten days, my connection with nature—particularly the birds—continued to deepen. They were my only source of connection during those days.

Let me tell you something. During those ten days, the birds took me everywhere I needed to go, showed me everything I needed to see, and told me everything I needed to know.

When you stop talking, you realize just how many other forms of communication there are in every person and in every animal. The universe doesn't speak English.

That's just one of the things I learned during those ten days. To be honest, this is the first time I'm sharing what happened during that meditation.

Frankly, nobody asked. That's the other thing I learned. I spent ten days not talking only to find out, nobody wanted to talk to me anyway.

When I started the no-talking meditation, I had no idea what would come of it. I had no idea that it would be the piece which would bring closure to my twenty-year journey of healing from being bullied.

Life Now

Let's start with Shady Palms Clubhouse. As I stated earlier, being angry at people for believing lies about me wasn't helping me win anyone over. After I relapsed for four days in the spring of 2023, I realized I needed to get away from the clubhouse. I couldn't recover from my addiction with a group of people who all thought I was a liar.

Honesty is the first step in recovery, and when no one believes a word you say, well, good luck with that!

During the two years that I was essentially living out of my car, sometimes staying at sober homes, and even for a few weeks staying at a men's shelter in Indio, I did briefly get an apartment in Yucca Valley and found some recovery at a place called the Alano Club.

In Yucca Valley, I connected with a new sponsor, Mike, who was also a painter and asked me if I wanted a job. I drove up to Yucca Valley everyday for over a year so that I could work and recover from my addiction.

Mike and the fellowship at the Alano Club in Yucca Valley saved my life. They took me in, welcomed me, and allowed me to be myself. Mike especially was incredibly patient and understanding, helping me work through many of the issues that brought me up there.

Mostly, they taught me how to "act" like a regular person. What I mean by that is, after I attended my first pride parade back in 1991, living my life became a political act. I carried my homosexuality in a very "in your face" kind of way.

We used to say a chant during pride rallies: "We're here, we're queer, get used to it!" That's how I lived my life.

I was gay and everyone had to know it and accept it. To me, that's what I considered "living out loud." Everywhere I went, I was like a one-man walking pride parade.

The truth is, most people don't appreciate that, although I have found most people (regardless of their age) don't care if you're gay or straight. What they don't appreciate is having it thrown in their face. And that was my problem.

The folks in Yucca Valley didn't care that I was gay, as long as I could sit there and participate in the meeting just like everyone else.

Believe me, when I got that straight love and acceptance, it healed me in a way that no gay man could ever heal me, no matter how rich or fabulous he might be. I believe gay people can't heal other gay people from our issues around straight acceptance. My experience was that straight people had created the most pain and suffering for me as a child. Therefore, only straight people could provide the healing I needed to recover from that hurt.

After my first year clean from crystal meth, I was offered a job back at Santiago, and I was beginning to find painting jobs in Palm Springs. That's when I started going back to

Shady Palms Clubhouse. At the writing of this memoir, I am secretary of the Tuesday 7:00 a.m. meeting—the very meeting I used to attend for years feeling like an outcast. The guys there have embraced me in a way they never have before. And yes, I still see the guy in the morning meeting who threw that rock at my car, and he gives me a hug every time I see him.

Now you may be wondering, how could I do that? There are a few reasons why I don't hold a grudge against that individual. First of all, this guy threw a rock at a homeless person's car. That's pretty ruthless, to say the least. I consider harassing the homeless to be akin to abusing animals. It's just downright despicable behavior. That's not the kind of person I want as my enemy.

Second, I know I did nothing wrong to this individual. I have given this person no reason to hate me and I'm certainly not going to do it now that I know what he is capable of doing. I know this person was performing someone else's dirty work, and I know that person was Frau DuLent. My experience with Frau has been that she is so cunning in her duplicity with me, I know I couldn't have been the first person she treated that way. If she did it to me, it's only a matter of time before she does it again. And when she does, I want those people to know that they are not alone. I keep my arms open, so those individuals won't feel isolated.

And third, the program we participate in has a code of love and tolerance. I have no choice but to be tolerant of these individuals as long as they are in the room with me. I am friendly. I am kind. I keep my distance, yet I remain open.

Obviously, some people probably still believe the lies, but I don't care. As long as those people continue to believe the lies and support the individuals who started them, they will never be my friend. And that's okay!

Not everyone is meant to be my friend. I learned that from my father when I told him I'd been arrested and the individual who had me arrested sent that video out to everyone I knew. He told me, "This is how you're going to find out who your friends are." Because, he said, the people who choose to believe the lies are not your friends.

It turned out, back then, I didn't have any friends in Palm Springs. It seemed like everyone believed what they were being told. Once I got to Yucca Valley, that's where I learned what it meant to be a friend.

By the time I got to Yucca Valley, the list of people who didn't like me was incredibly long. And the list of people who did like me was, well, that list was nonexistent. I mean, even I wasn't on that list. You understand what I'm saying.

Today, I can gratefully say that the list of people who like me is growing, and most importantly, I'm finally on that list. That's what's most important to me; the other list, I don't care about. I know there will always be people on that list. Not everyone is going to like me, and the reason I know that is because I don't like everybody. How could I expect anything different?

Wrap it Up

So, what happened with that court case? Adam's dodging the prosecutor's phone calls wasn't the only thing that delayed my case. I was arrested during the Covid pandemic, and because the courts closed, an extensive backlog of cases had to be heard before mine. Month after month, I would show up to court only to find out the California state legislature had extended my right to a fair trial by another thirty days.

One month, I remember my attorney, who happened to be licensed in both the states of New York and California, mentioned that there was no backlog of cases in New York. The courts in New York hadn't closed for the pandemic. "Aha," I said, "and that right there is the quintessential difference between east coast and west coast. In New York, justice is served no matter what, and in California, if you want justice you gotta fill out a form and get in line." That's California justice. You better be ready to wait.

And I did. For almost two years I showed up every month until the legislature could no longer extend my right to a fair trial. In early November of 2022, over two years after my arrest, my case was dropped. It wasn't the dismissal or vindication I'd hoped for, but it was over, and I was happy to be relieved of that burden. Now my recovery could really begin.

***

What about the word "faggot?" One of my greatest fears throughout my adult life was being called a "faggot." Hearing the word out of anyone's mouth would cause a painful visceral reaction in my gut. It hurt so deeply. So, I decided I needed to own it.

I needed to take the word and make myself so comfortable with it that no one would ever be able to hurt me with it again. I'll give you an example.

When I was attending meetings in Yucca Valley and was trying to figure out how to act right, I asked my friend Tommy a favor. I said, "Hey, Tommy, if you see me acting like a big faggot, just say, 'Hey, David, stop acting like a big faggot.'" And he did!

When he finally called me a faggot, I laughed and gave him a big hug. I said, "Thank you!"

I can't explain it, but when he said that, I was healed. All the power of that word went away in that instant, and it's never come back to me since.

***

When I began this journey into understanding the long-term consequences of being bullied, I didn't know if it would be possible to be healed from it. Now I know that it is possible to recover from having been bullied and take your life back.

I didn't know what recovery would look like. When I first googled the "long-term consequences of bullying," I didn't find much. No tools. No answers. No guides for how I would investigate my life. I made my own path on this journey of recovery to heal the wounds I carried as a result of being bullied.

I started with an honest inquiry into my own life and looked at how being bullied impacted my adult life in the long term. Once I chose to take responsibility for allowing it to happen, (after all I never told anyone, I never complained about it, and I never fought back) I was then able to forgive myself and once I forgave myself, then I could forgive my bullies. I did the work required to face my fears, let go of my anger, uncover the buried emotions, and release them. That was not easy work, but it was totally worth it!

Today I am free. I am free from the shame and guilt of that horrific experience. I no longer carry the burden of hatred that was cast upon me by other innocent children.

Today I am happy. I have serenity, love, and peace of mind. Those are things we all want. Those are things you can't buy in a store. Those are things that no one can give you. You can only give those gifts to yourself. They are within you. You need only find them.

Today I know myself. Looking within, I found all the answers to every question I ever had. It's all inside. You are the solution. You simply have to listen for it.

Today I see the world as a loving, kind place. Sure, I'm not naïve. I know evil exists among us, but I'm not looking for it.

When I see it, I move past it. I don't allow it to bother me. I'm not here to change the world; I'm here to change myself.

I live my life the way I choose and allow others to have the same privilege. My story is not unique. There are millions of others who've been bullied and there will be millions more. I don't think we will ever stop kids from bullying other kids. It's part of human nature. Period.

The best we can do is provide a supporting environment for those who were bullied. Open the conversation for those of us to talk about our experiences and heal from it. That's all it really takes. The first step is admitting you were bullied, then recognizing the long-term consequences and understanding you can recover.

I hope this book can open the conversation so that others feel comfortable talking about their experiences being bullied and honestly examine how it has impacted their lives.

You *can* take your life back!

Acknowledgment

First, thank you to Landmark Education. Participating in your coursework was a life-changing experience. It opened my mind to new ways of thinking and provided me with the technology necessary to let go of my past.

Next, I want to thank all my employees who ever worked under me as a retail manager. Thank you for putting up with all my bullshit. I apologize for mistreating you, disrespecting you and for any harm my actions may have caused.

I also want to thank Walt Disney for bringing the characters of Cinderella, Snow White, and Mary Poppins to life in compelling movie images and with song. Those characters taught me as a child that, by staying positive and being kind, I could survive some of the most harrowing experiences of my life.

Additionally, I want to thank Cher, Madonna, Whitney, and Mariah. Your voices and lyrics have carried me through all the challenging moments of my life, inspired me to believe in myself, and empowered me to be my own hero.

I also want to thank my Uncle Ronny for being a positive male role model, but most importantly for teaching me how to find the humor in life and to laugh, no matter how bad it gets.

I also want to thank my father for his advice on how to know who my friends are and for being a badass. I want to thank my mother for teaching me how to be a hard worker, and for showing me how to take care of myself. A special thanks to my Aunt Pearl for her unwavering financial support while I've lived in California, and to my entire family for their love, support, and generosity. Thank you for making me the man I am today.

My story would not be possible without the many bullies I've experienced in my life, both in-person and online. Thank you for your seemingly endless harassment, stalking, verbal abuse, and threats. Without you, I would not be who I am today!

I also want to thank the "mean gays" at Shady Palms Clubhouse for making me feel unwelcome and unwanted. Thanks to you, I was able to find the recovery and acceptance I needed from the straight community.

Thank you to my boss, Kent Taylor at Santiago, for always believing in me and showing me how to be a positive gay role model!

Thank you to my friend and "mom" Tracy Flynn for the care, love and support you have shown me.

Finally, I want to thank Johnathan Fast, PhD, for working with me to help shape the beginning of the book and for his contributions to the field of research on bullying.

www.ingramcontent.com/pod-product-compliance
Lightning Source LLC
LaVergne TN
LVHW052340100826
845147LV00021B/1133

* 9 7 8 1 9 5 4 6 0 4 1 8 6 *